# The Privatization of Schooling

Dedicated to

John W. Osborne

&

The Farm Girl

# The Privatization of Schooling

## Problems and Possibilities

### Joseph Murphy

CORWIN PRESS, INC.
A Sage Publications Company
Thousand Oaks, California

Copyright © 1996 Corwin Press, Inc.

*For information address:*

 SAGE Publications, Inc.
2455 Teller Road
Thousand Oaks, California 91320
E-mail: order@sagepub.com

SAGE Publications Ltd.
6 Bonhill Street
London EC2A 4PU
United Kingdom

SAGE Publications Pvt. Ltd.
M-32 Market
Greater Kailash I
New Delhi 110 048 India

Printed in the United States of America

**Library of Congress Cataloging-in-Publication Data**

Murphy, Joseph, 1949-
    The privatization of schooling: Problems and possibilities /
author, Joseph Murphy.
      p.  cm.
    Includes bibliographical references and index.
    ISBN 0-8039-6393-9 (cloth: acid-free paper). —
ISBN 0-8039-6394-7 (pbk.: acid-free paper)
    1. Privatization in education—United States.  I. Title.
LB2806.36.M87   1996
379.3'0973—dc20                  96-4523

This book is printed on acid-free paper.

96  97  98  99   10  9  8  7  6  5  4  3  2  1

Corwin Production Editor:  Gillian Dickens
Corwin Typesetter:  Janelle LeMaster

# CONTENTS

# ABOUT THE AUTHOR

**Joseph Murphy** is Professor and Chair in the Department of Educational Leadership at Peabody College of Vanderbilt University. He is also Vice-President of Division A of AERA and Chair of the Interstate School Leaders Licensure Consortium. Murphy's primary interest is in school improvement, with an emphasis on the role of policy. Recent volumes in this area include *School Based Management as School Reform: Taking Stock* (with Lynn G. Beck), *Restructuring Schools: Capturing and Assessing the Phenomena*, and *The Educational Reform Movement of the 1980s: Perspectives and Cases*.

Continuous resurveying of the border between government and private activity is necessary. (Tullock, 1994b, p. 78)

Today a broad and growing consensus recognizes that privatization, properly implemented, is a viable and legitimate response to a wide range of philosophical and practical concerns. . . . Consequently, privatization is likely to exert a powerful influence over the shape of political and economic institutions in coming years. (Miller & Tufts, 1991, p. 99)

Unfortunately, consideration of privatization alternatives often proceeds without a clear understanding of the concept under scrutiny or any evidence upon which proponents and opponents base their conclusions. (Van Horn, 1991, p. 261)

Theoretical arguments and empirical research both deserve attention and debate. (Gormley, 1991a, p. 4)

# SETTING THE STAGE | 1

Scholars and practitioners disagree sharply on the merits of contracting out. (Gormley, 1991b, p. 312)

The anecdotes are endless, and each has its own seemingly unequivocal conclusion. Privatization of public services is either the greatest innovation in government management since Benjamin Franklin's first American fire company or an insidious means of destroying the public work force. (Darr, 1991, p. 60)

Whether you want to prove that public ownership is good and private ownership is bad, or vice versa, there is a constant and abundant supply of triumphs and scandals to bolster your case. (Martin, 1993, p. 7)

As one becomes enmeshed in the privatization literature, it does not take much time to conclude that "views about privatization's virtues and pitfalls . . . vary widely" (Hirsch, 1991, p. 123). On one hand, we hear from proponents who maintain that privatization is the cure for the acute economic and political problems that confront many nations, states, and localities:

This book arrives at the position that privatization is the key to both limited and better government: limited in its size, scope, and power relative to society's other institutions; and better in that society's needs are satisfied more efficiently, effectively, and equitably. (Savas, 1987, p. 288)

The conviction grew that virtually any programme performed in the private economy could be done more efficiently, more cheaply, and with greater satisfaction to its beneficiaries than its counterpart could achieve in the public sector. (Pirie, 1988, p. 11)

Some advocates of this approach . . . have suggested an almost limitless application of this method for the production of public goods and services. (Wilson, 1990, p. 67)

Inspecting the same phenomenon, skeptics reach a completely different conclusion. They maintain that "public ownership . . . is not the uniform disaster that the privatization movement makes it out to be" (Starr, 1991, p. 30), and they view privatization initiatives with a more jaundiced eye than do proponents:

The advocates of privatization have succeeded in focusing attention on some serious problems of public expenditure and public management. Those problems need our attention, but privatization is not a general solution to them. (Starr, 1991, p. 34)

It is thus not surprising that the "privatization" of public service delivery—in such forms as "contracting out" services or "public-private partnerships"—is best translated as conspiracies to loot the public treasury. (Thayer, 1987, p. 147)

Those observing from still other vantage points form opinions somewhere between those of the proponents and those of the skeptics:

While there are many merits in the argument for privatization, neither theoretical arguments nor empirical evidence presently provide a compelling basis for urging full speed ahead. The current signals are blinking yellow. (Pack, 1991, pp. 304-305)

Thus, we have a movement that

> in the eyes of some is the cure for an anemic, inefficient econ-
> omy; in the eyes of others, privatization is bad medicine that
> hurts workers, interferes with real accountability to consum-
> ers, and prevents women and other minorities from climbing
> up the social ladder. (Hirsch, 1991, p. 123)

> While privatization advocates have aggressively advanced
> it as the solution to public social service fiscal, administra-
> tive and political dilemmas, its antagonists have as aggres-
> sively attacked it as an erosion of the principles of universal-
> ity and equity in the social service delivery system. (Ismael
> & Vaillancourt, 1988, p. vii)

It is important to remember that these disparate reviewers may
not come to the analysis encumbered with deep-seated beliefs and
values about the phenomenon under scrutiny. In addition, they often
employ different yardsticks to measure the salutary or harmful
effects of privatization. Even when they use similar criteria, the
weights they apply to these standards often vary. Equally important,
the complexity of privatization encourages analysts to break off
manageable pieces of the puzzle for inspection. Reviewers studying
these discrete parts can fall prey to what Starr (1987) labels "heroically selective attention" (p. 128). Thus, "advocates of more or less
privatization frequently talk past one another because they are talking about different phenomena" (Van Horn, 1991, p. 261). Finally,
because privatization involves "gainers and losers" (Bell & Cloke,
1990, p. 24), how one, or one's reference group, is affected may shape
the frames used in analysis.

Our intention throughout this volume is to help readers who are
"bombarded with conflicting advice by privatizers and their opponents" (Worsnop, 1992, p. 981) to develop more refined lenses for
viewing the privatization movement as it begins to sweep over public education. Because we agree with Martin (1993) that "tit for tat
trading" (p. 7) of anecdotes and stories will lead us nowhere, our
work is synthetic and suggestive rather than actuarial or polemical.
We start with Clarkson's (1989) simple but elegant principle that "a
vital part of any privatization effort is to fully understand the concept" (p. 180). Our intent is not to join one camp or another but rather

to review privatization "in real [as well as] ideological terms to see its actual utility" (Bailey, 1987, p. 143). We paint a "broad canvas" because only by treating "the historical, conceptual and practical roots of privatisation" (Bell & Cloke, 1990, p. 4) can the idea be thoroughly understood. Given the likely expansion of privatization initiatives, our ultimate goal is to "improve our odds of getting more of the right kind of privatization, and less of the wrong kind" in education (Donahue, 1989, p. 13).

## An Initial Glimpse of Roadblocks

The United States is experiencing a renewed interest in the systematic examination of the boundary between public and private delivery of goods and services. (President's Commission on Privatization, 1988, p. 1)

It is being argued (at least implicitly) that the processes of decision and implementation in government can be subjected to the standards of the market. In short, the possibility has been raised that public management can be privatized. (Baber, 1987, p. 153)

Privatization is, to put it mildly, a "hot topic" in the economic, political, and managerial realms of public service provision—"much in discussion and highly controversial" (Kolderie, 1991, p. 250). The ideology of privatization has, according to Hardin (1989), descended on the debate about public service "like a low-flying fog" (p. 4). "All across the country, state and local officials—liberals and conservatives alike—are jumping aboard the privatization bandwagon" (Worsnop, 1992, p. 979). In particular, there is growing interest in the application of privatization to the social services (Savas, 1987).

### Complexity

Privatization is a relatively recent phenomenon (Kuttner, 1991): "While the private marketplace has been in existence since the beginning of time, it has only recently begun to provide public services" (Kemp, 1991, p. 1). Although it "may well be seen by future historians as one of the most important developments in American political and economic life of the late 20th century" (President's Commission on Privatization, 1988, p. 251), its effects are "only beginning to be felt" (p. 251) today. There is a good deal more to be learned.

Privatization means different things to different people (Florestano, 1991), and it can unfold in a variety of settings. It represents a complex cultural, political, legal, and economic equation (Bell & Cloke, 1990). It has political, technical, strategic, and ideological dimensions. It comes in a myriad of forms, from asset sales to vouchers. Privatization is proposed as a strategy to meet an almost limitless set of objectives, from shrinking the overall size of government to enhancing the technical efficiency of specific public sector services. For some, it is an end in itself; for others, it is the means to other valued outcomes (Savas, 1987). "Nothing [about the process of privatization] is either certain or clear-cut" (Darr, 1991, p. 60). The implementation of privatization may not conform to the ideal (De Hoog, 1984). In particular, "the complexity of implementation may make the promise of private production difficult and costly to achieve" (Pack, 1991, p. 288). Unexpected—and often unwanted—consequences abound.

## Ideology

One of the most troubling aspects of privatization is the extent to which the "discussion of government activities runs instantaneously into a barrier of very strongly held ideas" (Tullock, 1988, p. 70). In particular, "arguments [for or against it] are often advanced by special interest groups" (Hirsch, 1991, p. 65). Another is the extent to which analysts have cloaked themselves in the mantle of ideology. The debate has been "fundamentally ideological" (Ismael & Vaillancourt, 1988, p. vii), undertaken by "acolytes" (Hardin, 1989, p. 5) on the left and right imbued with an "ideological fervor" (De Hoog, 1984, p. 15), "hurling political slogans back and forth" (Van Horn, 1991, p. 261):

The very word *privatization* unfortunately summons forth images from a deep reservoir and causes misunderstanding, premature polarization, and shrill arguments that are beside the point more often than not. (Savas, 1987, p. 277)

Current arguments in favor of privatization and, for that matter, in opposition to it, often appear to be ideology-based. Conservatives in general and businesses in particular tend to advance positive arguments; liberals in general and labor in particular are strongly opposed. (Hirsch, 1991, p. 11)

As the privatisation programme has gathered pace, however, it has taken on many of the characteristics of an ideology, with actual evidence as to the effects of the various initiatives being seen as irrelevant (the claims to universal benefits automatically and necessarily being correct, and alternatives being dismissed brusquely). Any merits attributed to the public sector, in particular, have been howled down. (Bell & Cloke, 1990, p. 8)

As a result, although both sides address relevant issues, they often "do so in a highly lopsided manner and possibly incorrectly" (Hirsch, 1991, p. 65).

## Context

Equally troubling, and of critical importance in this volume as we examine implications for education, is the fact that "the political and organizational contexts of contracting out have been largely ignored in the empirical research" (De Hoog, 1984, p. 11). Despite acknowledgments that the "resolution of the assignment problem is site specific" (Ross, 1988, p. xiv)—that "the feasibility of privatization should be determined on a site specific basis" (Goldman & Mokuvos, 1991, p. 26)—unanchored cross-locality (Hemming & Mansoor, 1988) and cross-sector (Bell & Cloke, 1990; Donahue, 1989) claims are commonplace in the literature. As we ponder the application of privatization concepts to education, it is important to remember that no universal assertions are possible (Donahue, 1989), and that lessons from one sector of activity must be applied with caution to other public services: "What works in one place or in one circumstance doesn't necessarily work somewhere else" (Darr, 1991, p. 60):

It is dangerous to generalize as to the success of privatization options. There will be situations where a switch will be worthwhile and cases where it won't be. . . . The appropriateness and success of using a particular privatization option is *highly situational*. Success depends on many factors that are individual to the particular public agency, in the particular location and at the particular time. (Hatry, 1991, pp. 264, 266)

## Assessment

Much of what we have described above casts a long shadow over assessments of privatization initiatives. Many of the studies are "based on small and unsystematic sets of observations and on relatively primitive methodologies" (Donahue, 1989, p. 133). This work "invite[s] ideological rivals to brandish equally dubious statistical studies demonstrating the opposite point" (Donahue, 1989, p. 133). This trading of stories (Martin, 1993) or "argument by anecdote and . . . selective statistics" (Donahue, 1989, p. 133), although common, is not particularly helpful.

Even when higher quality studies are available, the assessment of privatization remains problematic. Evaluations often play out outside "the grand ideology and narrow electoral calculations [that] form an inescapable backdrop against which privatisation must be assessed" (Bell & Cloke, 1990, p. 8; Bailey, 1987). Concomitantly, although it is desirable that "*inquiry* into privatization . . . be multidisciplinary in nature . . . much of the privatization debate has focused on cost containment—the province of economics" (Gormley, 1991a, p. 4): "Debates about the merits of privatization usually focus exclusively on the question of efficiency: is it cheaper to deliver a public service through a private vendor as opposed to a government agency?" (Van Horn, 1991, p. 262). Other relevant criteria for evaluating privatization—such as effectiveness, equity, and accountability —are often ignored (Ross, 1988). Thus, the larger and more relevant macrolevel criterion of "social efficiency" (Hirsch, 1991, p. 6) is subordinated to the issue of technical efficiency. Even when multiple criteria are brought to bear on privatization decisions, because "they are not all measured in the same units" (Ross, 1988, p. 19), analysts have a difficult time aggregating assessment findings. Finally, even when all goes well, empirical comparisons in this area "are messy, tentative and hedged about with conditions" (Donahue, 1989, p. 57). All of this argues for caution in generalizing the work on privatization to education.

## Conclusion

A central theme of this volume is that the use of privatization strategies in education should proceed from an informed understanding of the strengths and weaknesses as well as the goals and objectives of this particular bundle of policy instruments. In this chapter, we began our journey to develop a deeper understanding of privatization, looking specifically at an array of factors that have the potential to cloud our ability to see this phenomenon clearly. In the next chapter, we continue our quest to develop a clear understanding of this array of policy tools by analyzing the objectives of privatization and by examining the strands of activities that define privatization.

# DEFINING PRIVATIZATION | 2

The privatization debate, as an exercise in institutional policy analysis, is part of a larger debate on how we should redesign our political, economic, and social institutions. (Gormley, 1991a, p. 15)

Privatization is both a means and an end. For pragmatists who want better government and for populists who seek a better society, privatization is a means toward those ends. The government that results from the practice of privatization is leaner and more adroit, and society is sturdier and more adaptable. For those who, on ideological grounds, seek to limit government, and for those who seek commercial opportunities in government work, privatization is an end in itself. (Savas, 1987, p. 288)

The techniques available to the advocate of privatization are extensive. (Butler, 1987, p. 13)

In the first part of this chapter, we continue our efforts to forge an understanding of privatization by reviewing definitions of the concept. We start by situating this emerging strategy in the larger context of downsizing and decentralizing government. We then examine why the concept, which appears so straightforward on the surface, is so difficult to pin down. Next, definitions of privatization are presented, and common elements are culled out. Finally, the critical distinction between the allocation (financing) and production (distribution) of goods and services is introduced. The second part of the chapter provides an overview of the major goals of privatization. The third part lays out an approach for developing a comprehensive understanding of privatization—a taxonomy of strategies employed to shift the allocation and/or production of functions from the public to the private sector.

## Definitions

Privatization is a new word that is rapidly coming into popular usage despite its awkward sound. The word *privatize* first appeared in a dictionary in 1983 and was defined narrowly as "to make private, especially to change (as a business or industry) from public to private control or ownership." (Savas, 1987, p. 3)

In fact, all we are really talking about with privatization is making the private sector available, in some form, for achieving public objectives. (Butler, 1991, p. 24)

### A Piece of a Larger Mosaic

Privatization may be identified as part of a broader process of devolution of responsibility for social provision. (Ismael, 1988, p. 1)

The privatization movement is part of a larger landscape of reform. On one hand, it is an element in a long cyclical pattern in which the appeal of markets is tarnished by market failures and the perceived need for more public services and in which the putative inefficiencies of the public sector in turn cause market solutions to shine more brightly again. At the current time, for many, the luster of governmental services has tarnished. Today, we hear many calls for a reconfiguring "of the structure of the welfare state" (Ismael, 1988, p. 1; Donahue, 1989). There is a "broad trend represent[ing] a return to a more residual model of welfare provision" (Ismael, 1988, p. 1)—"redistribution through taxation and budgeting [is]

becoming a less attractive policy" (Bailey, 1987, p. 138) for governments. Thus, as the President's Commission on Privatization (1988)
informs us:

> Privatization is much more than a set of specific changes in
> who performs an activity and how. It is part of a fundamen-
> tal political and economic rethinking that today is reassess-
> ing the roles of government and the private sector in the
> modern welfare state—a rethinking that is having an influ-
> ence on all segments of American opinion. (p. xii)

According to some analysts, "it is time to pursue other paths [than
public provision] toward the desired objective of social well-being"
(Savas, 1987, p. 234).

It is also useful to remind ourselves that privatization is only one
of many "off-budget policy instruments" (Bailey, 1987, p 138) employed in the quest to restrain the costs of and/or downsize government and to restore the benefits of markets. As Hemming and
Mansoor (1988) state, "The poor performance of public enterprises
can be tackled in a variety of ways, and privatization is not the first
to be tried" (p. 6). "Government officials have adopted a number of
strategies in the face of this altered political atmosphere" (Florestano,
1991, p. 292).

Many of the nonprivatization measures—or "market analogs"
(Hula, 1990b, p. 8)—designed to rein in government spending emanate from reformers who "concede the failures of public bureaucracies but [who] argue that the performance of public bureaucracies
can be improved through institutional redesign" (Gormley, 1991a,
p. 6). They focus on experimentation "with innovative public management techniques to cut ongoing costs without cutting service
benefits" (Moore, 1987, p. 61)—with "statutory and administrative
measures to control public enterprises" (Hemming & Mansoor, 1988,
p. 6). "In this instance policy development and implementation is not
necessarily turned over to the private sector, but rather an effort is
made to replicate the conditions in markets thought to generate
desired social outcomes" (Hula, 1990b, p. 8).

Miller and Tufts (1991) describe four such alternatives: "productivity and quality improvement programs, consolidation (intra- and
inter-government cooperation), program reduction, [and] program
abandonment" (p. 98). Moore (1987) lists two related strategies: "co-

ordinating procurement policies with neighboring communities to take advantage of quantity discounts (a practice known as 'piggy backing'), and hiring outside management consultants to advise city officials on cutting costs" (p. 62). Hilke (1992) also outlines two methods "of subjecting . . . public sector organizations to management ideologies and practices derived from the private sector" (Bell & Cloke, 1990, p. 9): intergovernmental competition in which there is competition between government jurisdictions and interagency competition in which two or more agencies within a jurisdiction "compete against each other in the manner of private firms" (Hilke, 1992, p. 19). Bailey (1991) argues that all the following approaches can be gathered under the umbrella of alternative methods of promoting fiscal restraint within government agencies: "strategic planning, land-use planning, exactive zoning, community-sponsored public benefit corporations, public development corporations, public-private partnerships" (p. 233). Gormley (1991a) describes the following approaches to enhance the performance of the public sector: providing greater accountability to consumers "through greater consumer choice or clientele feedback" (p. 6); promoting greater accountability of bureaucrats and politicians; listening more attentively to the ideas of workers; decentralization, including "abandon[ing] hierarchical structures" (p. 6); analyzing policies more thoughtfully; and conducting audits.

According to Pirie (1988), several nonprivatization strategies

> have been used by governments to deal with the escalating costs of public programmes. All of them attempt in some measure to supply pressures which might oppose those already in operation. . . . The solutions which have been attempted have tried different ways to exert control by government in order that it can substitute its own priorities in place of those followed by the system itself. (pp. 39-40)

Among the most prevalent nonprivatization tactics are the following: efficiency drives, drives to eliminate waste, elimination of unnecessary programs, and cash limits.

*Efficiency drives.* As comparative studies bring to the attention of governments the inferior performance of public sector supply, the attempt is sometimes made to graft on to the public programme some of the efficiency-making expertise of the private sector. The theory behind the approach is that the private sector encourages its personnel to adopt efficient practices and teaches them the appropriate skills. Since the disciplines which have this effect are absent from the public sector, the expertise must be brought in from outside. In other words, those who have acquired those skills by experience in the private sector can be imported to the public sector to apply there what they have learned. (p. 40)

*Drives to eliminate waste.* An alternative tactic employed by a cost-conscious government is the initiation of procedures to identify and eliminate waste within public operations. If these really are practices which add to costs without contributing to the output, such as duplication or time-wasting activities, they can in theory be identified and removed. Because a department of the public sector can fall into established ways of doing things without questioning their basis, it is usually advantageous to bring in someone from outside to conduct the survey, on the grounds that they will be likely to see things which might not be obvious to insiders. (p. 42)

*Eliminating unnecessary programmes.* Governments seeking to cut taxes look for areas of public sector supply rendered obsolete and unnecessary by changing social circumstances. A body set up half a century ago might no longer be required, given the new levels of affluence. . . . A possible source of public sector saving might be found in the complete elimination of unnecessary services. (p. 44)

*Cash limits.* The cash limits strategy tries to do two things. By imposing an overall budget limit on a department, it encourages some areas within the department to oppose spending by others, since this is the only way their own can acquire additional funds. The hope is that in this way, essential services will be guaranteed but that administrators will join forces with each other to vote down increased appropriations to unnecessary activities. The second aim of a cash limits policy is that the administrators themselves will introduce efficiency and anti-waste campaigns to continue operation under the constraint of an overall limit on spend-

ing. Here too, the assumption is that what is not needed will
go, leaving an altogether more cost-effective programme.
(pp. 46-47)

It would be premature to leave this analysis without reporting
that privatization advocates are generally skeptical of the power of
these alternative "cost-cutting" strategies to reform the public sector.
For reasons that we describe in detail in later chapters—especially
what many see as inherent tendencies toward continual growth and
producer domination in the public sector (Pirie, 1988; Savas, 1987)—
they maintain that such initiatives have been and will continue to be
largely ineffectual. They lobby instead for a rebalancing of the public
market equation and for introducing privatization more forcefully
into the "political discourse" (Kuttner, 1991, p. 311). Thus, "considerable attention is now turning to the possibility of increasing private
sector involvement in public enterprises" (Hemming & Mansoor,
1988, p. 6).

### A Multilayered Construct

Privatization has several different meanings (Florestano, 1991,
p. 292). For a variety of reasons, it is a difficult idea to corral: "[It]
is not only an inelegant term; it is also lamentably imprecise"
(Donahue, 1989, p. 5). To begin with, "the concept itself is unclear"
(Bailey, 1987, p. 138). It is, as Butler (1991) reminds us, "a highly
varied" (p. 24) term. There really are "several different concepts of
'privatization'" (Bailey, 1987, p. 138). Quite "different ideas are being
expressed by the same use of the word" (Kolderie, 1991, p. 250). In
addition, rather diverse objectives often find sanctuary under the
same banner.

Some of the confusion over the meaning of privatization is due
to the newness of the concept (Florestano, 1991; Peters, 1991). Part is
also attributable to the fact that it is a "dynamic concept" (Savas,
1987, p. 88). And a good deal is caused by the fact that privatization
has become a "political weapon" (Bailey, 1987, p. 138), a condition
that drains concepts of clarity. "Privatization may look [from] afar
[fairly] straightforward. . . . From close in it can be seen as an array
of complex policies" (Pirie, 1988, p. 11).

One way of defining privatization is to listen to the voices of some of the leading scholars and practitioners in the area:

Privatization is the shifting of a function, either in whole or in part, from the public sector to the private sector. (Butler, 1991, p. 17)

Privatization . . . is the transfer of assets or service functions from public to private ownership or control. (Hanke, 1987, p. 2)

Privatization is the decision of a jurisdiction to curtail producing a service in-house in favor of production by an outside organization, usually a private one. (Hilke, 1992, p. 16)

In the broadest sense, privatization refers to the attainment of any public policy goal through the participation of the private sector. (Dudek & Company, 1989, p. 7)

At its lowest common denominator, it meant having done in the private sector that which previously had been done in the public sector. (Pirie, 1988, p. 9)

Privatization is the act of reducing the role of government, or increasing the role of the private sector, in an activity or in the ownership of assets. (Savas, 1987, p. 3)

Privatization refers to a shift from publicly to privately produced goods and services. (Starr, 1987, p. 125)

A somewhat more encompassing definition has been provided by De Alessi (1987):

The term *privatization* is typically used to describe the transfer of activities from the public sector to the private sector and includes contracting out as well as reducing or discontinuing the provision of some goods and services by government. More accurately, privatization entails a move toward private property and away from not only government and common ownership but also from government regulations that limit individual rights to the use of resources. (p. 24)

At the most basic level, two elements are common to these, and nearly all other, definitions of privatization—a movement away from reliance on government agencies to provide goods and services and a movement toward the private sector and market forces.

In an effort to foreshadow our discussion of types of privatization below and to bring greater depth to our analysis of the definition of privatization, it is useful to introduce the distinction between the allocation/financing of goods and services and the production/delivery/distribution of those goods and services:

> Allocation involves decisions about whether a given good or service should be offered, and if so, who should receive it, how much of it, and at what price. (Hirsch, 1991, p. 25)

> The term *distribution* is commonly used . . . to mean the activity carried out by the sellers to get the good or service to the consumer. (p. 25)

According to Savas (1987), this "distinction between providing or arranging a service and producing it is profound. It is at the heart of the entire concept of privatization and puts the role of government in perspective" (p. 61). Thus, in defining privatization,

> we cannot talk simply about a public sector and a private sector. Only a *four*-part concept of the sectors—combining providing and producing, government and non-government —will let us have a useful discussion about the roles of public and private and about the strategy of privatization. (Kolderie, 1991, p. 251)

For the purposes of this volume, it is important to point out that "the desirability of government action does not mean that the government should actually provide the service" (Tullock, 1994b, p. 77). In particular, Niskanen (1971) cautions analysts to "be particularly careful to distinguish between well-developed arguments for government financing of public services and the rather casual arguments for the bureaucratic supply of public services" (p. 9). "The decision about what goods to supply at collective expense is quite separate from the decision about what arrangement to use to deliver the goods" (Savas, 1987, p. 278).

## Objectives

Privatization may be undertaken for any of a wide range of purposes. (Hilke, 1992, p. 17)

Privatisation is thus supposed to achieve a great many things. (Bell & Cloke, 1990, p. 7)

To understand the concept of privatization, one must examine the goals of this policy framework. It is at this level—as well as during implementation—that much of the complexity of privatization becomes evident. Privatization is, according to its supporters, a policy tool designed to achieve an enormous array of goals. As Donahue (1989) relates,

the word can signify something as broad as shrinking the welfare state while promoting self-help and voluntarism, or something as narrow as substituting a team of private workers for an all-but-identical team of civil servants to carry out a particular task. (pp. 5-6)

We sketch the major goals of privatization below under the headings of Macro- and Microlevel Objectives. A fuller treatment is contained in Chapter 4, where we examine the case for and against privatization.

### Macrolevel Objectives

The privatization movement is about large ideas. (Pack, 1991, p. 281)

In privatization they believe they have found a sovereign remedy against all ailments to the body politic, good for stimulating economic growth, improving the efficiency of services, slimming down the state, and expanding individual freedom, including the opportunities of disadvantaged minorities, too. (Starr, 1987, p. 124)

Macrolevel goals refer to changes that are designed to both affect the larger political and economic structures of the nation and redefine the algorithm by which markets and governments address fundamental questions about the allocation and provision of goods and services. At this level, although the objectives of privatization vary, the most frequently cited goals include:

> (1) the improvement of the economic performance of the assets or service functions concerned; (2) the depoliticization of economic decisions; (3) the generation of public budget revenues through sale receipts; (4) the reduction in public outlays, taxes, and borrowing requirements; (5) the reduction in the power of public-sector unions; and (6) the promotion of popular capitalism through the wide ownership of assets. (Hanke, 1987, p. 2)

Some authors perceive privatization as a vehicle to help "restore government to its fundamental purpose to steer, not to man the oars" (Savas, 1987, p. 290). Others who view "privatization as part of a wider neo-liberal policy package" (Martin, 1993, p. 99) maintain that a key objective, for better or worse, is to reconstruct the "liberal democratic state" (Starr, 1991, p. 25), to redefine the operational "set of assumptions about the capacities of democratic government and the appropriate sphere of common obligation" (p. 25). Privatization here is viewed, in particular, as a vehicle to overcome the "dependency culture" (Martin, 1993, p. 48) associated with a social order dominated by government activity. Another aim is to depoliticize service operations (Hanke & Dowdle, 1987). As Pirie (1988) argues, "the actual transfer to the private sector . . . can take the service into the purely economic world and out of the political world . . . freeing it from the political forces which acted upon it in the state sector" (pp. 52-53) and overcoming "structural weaknesses inherent in the nature of public sector supply" (p. 20).

Perhaps the central purpose and most highly touted objective of privatization is "reduction in the size of the public sector" (Pack, 1991, p. 284), "reducing public spending and taxation as proportions of gross domestic product" (Hardin, 1989, p. 20). The goal is to "downsize or rightsize government" (Worsnop, 1992, p. 984). Based on the belief that government is too large and too intrusive and that "government's decisions are political and thus are inherently less trustworthy than free-market decisions" (Savas, 1982, p. 5), the focus is on "rolling back either the rate of growth or the absolute amount of state activity in the social service delivery system" (Ismael, 1988, p. 1).

Two highly related objectives deal with raising additional revenue (Hanke & Dowdle, 1987; Savas, 1982) and reducing the size of government debt (Hardin, 1989; Miller & Tufts, 1991), the latter issue taking on increased emphasis in the United States as the size of the deficit has grown (Pack, 1991).

A further objective is to enhance the overall health of the economy: "If reducing the size of the public sector is the dominant theme in the work of privatization advocates, enhancing the efficiency of the economy as a whole and the public sector in particular is their *leitmotif*" (Pack, 1991, p. 287). The sub-aims are to enhance "efficiency and responsiveness" (Bell & Cloke, 1990, p. 7); to promote "savings, investment, productivity, and growth" (Starr, 1987, p. 126); "to decrease the use of scarce resources" (Miller & Tufts, 1991, p. 100); to ensure that customers are "served more effectively" (Hanke & Dowdle, 1987, p. 115); and to promote cost effectiveness by "help[ing] get prices right" (Starr, 1991, p. 32). Related to the issue of cost effectiveness is still another objective of privatization—"to reduce the power of public sector trade unions" (Hardin, 1989, p. 30) and thereby to exercise "control of wage rates" (Bell & Cloke, 1990, p. 7).

Finally, privatization is often portrayed as a tactic for promoting "choice in public services" (Savas, 1987, p. 5): "The key word is *choice*. Advocates claim that privatization will enlarge the range of choice for individuals while serving the same essential functions as do traditional programs" (Starr, 1987, p. 131). According to Gormley (1991b) and other analysts, "privatization enable[s] individual consumers to pursue their private choices more freely" (p. 309). These same analysts further posit that "greater freedom of choice will generally lead to a more just distribution of benefits" (Starr, 1987, p. 131), serve the interest of equity, and promote democracy (Bell & Cloke, 1990; Thayer, 1987).

## Microlevel Objectives

The overriding motivation for contracting out is to cut the cost of providing government services. (Dudek & Company, 1989, p. 1)

Macrolevel goals are designed to affect the larger economic and political infrastructure of society. The microlevel goals of privatization focus on improvements in a particular government function or set of functions. The major objective here is enhanced efficiency, most often expressed in terms of reduced costs. Other related outcomes sought through moving functions from the public realm to the private sphere include overcoming "limitations of staff and expertise" (Van Horn, 1991, p. 271) in the public sector; better quality, defined in terms of effectiveness and reliability; greater flexibility and reduced taxpayer risk; additional consumer choice; more effective accountability; and enhanced citizen participation.

## Types

Privatization, as practiced in the United States, follows no single pattern. (Worsnop, 1992, p. 979)

The techniques available to the advocate of privatization are extensive and sophisticated. (Butler, 1987, p. 13)

The blanket term "privatisation" covers a variety of different trends and initiatives in various different sectors. It is, however, possible to disaggregate the idea into a number of conceptual schemes of varying degrees of complexity. (Bell & Cloke, 1990, p. 8)

Privatization is not only intended to meet quite diverse objectives, but it also comes in a variety of forms. It is a "highly complex process which unpacks into a plethora of individual initiatives" (Bell & Cloke, 1990, p. 9). As Starr (1991) observes,

The term covers a heterogeneous package of measures, including: 1) governmental disengagement from a function, as in the cessation of a program; 2) the sale or lease of assets, such as land, infrastructure, or state-owned enterprises; 3) the replacement of publicly produced services with public payments for private services, through contracts, vouchers, or cost-plus reimbursement; or 4) some forms of deregulation that open up an industry to private competition, where previously public institutions were the only legal providers. (p. 26)

In this section, I present my typology of the most important forms of privatization. Although my classification system draws heavily upon the writings of all the major contributors to the privatization literature, I am particularly in the debt of Donahue (1989), Hirsch (1991), Pirie (1985), and Savas (1982, 1987).

Before defining these "policy initiatives" (Bailey, 1991, p. 234), "methods" (Fixler & Poole, 1991, p. 70), "forms" (Butler, 1991, p. 18), "arrangements" (Savas, 1987, p. 88), "techniques" (Clarkson, 1989, p. 144), or "strands" (Bell & Cloke, 1990, p. 10) of privatization, a few notes are in order. First, although there are many forms of privatization and although "no one of them excludes the others" (Bailey, 1987, p. 139), there are distinct tensions among them (Bell & Cloke, 1990). Second, particular types of privatization tend to be more prevalent in specific social service areas (e.g., contracting out in public services and franchising in public utilities) (Fixler & Poole, 1991). Third, although the separation of activities between the public and private sectors is central to analysis in this area, the distinction is "a good deal messier" (Donahue, 1989, p. 8) than it is often portrayed. Thus, "comparisons of public and private forms of organization must be either hedged about with qualifications, or taken as slightly artificial statements of tendency" (p. 9).

There is no shortage of lists of privatization schemes, ranging from the two basic forms described by Hirsch (1991)—permanent and temporary privatization—to the 22 methods detailed by Pirie (1988). Similarly, a variety of criteria are employed to classify privatization techniques, including, most commonly, (a) the extent of privatization—"from the most complete to the least complete" (Butler, 1991, p. 18); (b) the domain of activity involved—usually financing and production; and (c) the place in the delivery of the service where privatization takes root—policy, administration, or provision. In Figure 2.1, we provide a typology of the significant forms of privatization based upon these criteria. The objective of privatization is to replace activities in Quadrant 1 (government services), in which "the government that finances provision of the service actually produces the service" (Hilke, 1992, p. 3), with more market-based allocation and distribution strategies. In Figure 2.1, movements from the top to the bottom and from the left to the right

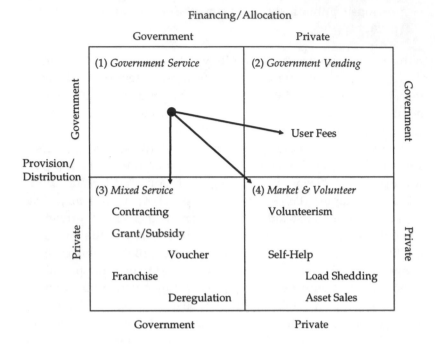

**Figure 2.1.** A Typology of Privatization Initiatives—by Extent and Domain

represent "higher degree(s) of privatization" (Savas, 1987, p. 88). The remainder of this section defines each of the 10 strategies graphed in Figure 2.1: load shedding, asset sales, volunteerism, self-help, user fees, contracting, grants/subsidies, franchises, vouchers, and deregulation.

### Load Shedding

> Load shedding eliminates government financing and production of a particular service and lets the private sector take over the function, if a private market develops. (Pack, 1991, p. 283)

Privatization via load shedding occurs when a government unit withdraws from the provision of an existing service. Also referred to as "disestablishment" (Thompson, 1989, p. 203) and "service-shedding" (Clarkson, 1989, p. 145), load shedding is the "oldest notion of privatization" (Bailey, 1991, p. 234). It is also the "most radical" (Peters, 1991, p. 53), one of the most controversial (Fixler, 1991), and the most likely to garner significant cost savings (Clarkson, 1989; Fixler, 1991). Load shedding comes in three forms: "shedding to for-profit firms, shedding to nonprofit organizations, and straight discontinuance" (Clarkson, 1989, p. 150). An implicit form of divestiture occurs when the government "provides tax incentives to neighborhoods . . . to forgo certain services" (Fixler, 1991, p. 41). According to Savas (1987), load shedding can be "carried out by divestiture, default, and accommodation" (p. 233). It is also important to note that governments have at their disposal a variety of incentives—"tax rebates, credits, and reductions, as well as appropriate deregulation" (Fixler, 1991, p. 41)—to induce private sector participation in jettisoned government services (Fixler, 1991).

Examples of load shedding at the local level include the withdrawal from the commercial trash collection business by the City of Knoxville, Tennessee (Fitzgerald, Lyons, & Cory, 1990) and the abandonment of municipal solid-waste collection services in Wichita, Kansas (Fixler, 1991). Using the data from the International City Management Association study, Fixler (1991) shows that nearly one in four (23.9%) local government units has shed one or more services recently, of which 56.3% were taken over by for-profit and nonprofit organizations, with the balance being discontinued. Examples of load shedding in education include the elimination of transportation services, advanced language classes, and cocurricular activities.

### Asset Sales

Another method of privatization is asset divestiture, where the public sector sells an asset, such as government land holdings, to the private sector to generate revenue and/or to spur private sector development. (Dudek & Company, 1989, p. 7)

The third definition—one recently added to the nuances of privatization—is the sale of assets. . . . What is really being proposed in these "privatizations" is the liquidation of assets for their cash value. (Bailey, 1991, p. 235)

Closely related to initiatives to shed services are efforts at privatization that involve "removing . . . assets from the collective realm" (Donahue, 1989, p. 216)—"changing the public-private balance . . . by moving state-owned enterprises into private ownership" (Starr, 1991, p. 30). Activities in this area are often bundled together under the heading of denationalization. Although "asset divestiture is probably the most controversial" (Seader, 1991, p. 33) of the privatization arrangements, as well as the most popular in much of the world (Dudek & Company, 1989; Hardin, 1989), it is the least active form in the United States (Seader, 1991), "primarily because many of the functions now being privatized in other countries have traditionally been in the private sector in this country" (Butler, 1991, p. 18). In education, the sale of an unused school facility to a corporation or volunteer agency would be an example of an asset sale.

### Volunteerism

> As a privatization strategy, the use of volunteers generally refers to the recruitment of individuals to work for government without remuneration, thereby reducing the degree of tax-supported involvement by government in the provision of public services. (Clarkson, 1989, p. 148)

> As always, private individuals, prompted by moral considerations and acting through voluntary charitable associations, proved able and willing to help those less fortunate than themselves and thereby assumed a portion of the social burden amassed by government. (Savas, 1987, p. 237)

Privatization through volunteerism refers to situations in which government-like services are financed and delivered privately but without the use of traditional market mechanisms. "Volunteers have been used extensively in the provision of various public-safety services . . . [and] volunteers are a major resource in the provision of recreational, parks, and cultural arts programs" (Clarkson, 1989, p. 148). Although the link between volunteerism and privatization is often not drawn, Savas (1987) reminds us that "when a voluntary association engages in the business of supplying private goods, such as a housing or food cooperative, it is no different from a private, nonprofit firm operating in the free market" (p. 80). Examples of volunteerism in education are legion and include everything from room parents to unpaid volunteer instructors.

### Self-Help

Self-help is the most underutilized privatization alternative. Under this approach, the government encourages individuals or groups to provide their own services; that is, the individuals involved become their own clients. (Clarkson, 1989, p. 148)

Self-help, "the most basic delivery mode of all" (Savas, 1987, p. 81), has a good deal in common with voluntary forms of privatization. A critical difference is that with self-help strategies, those who provide the services are the direct beneficiaries (Clarkson, 1989). Fitzgerald (1988), Gormley (1991a), and Savas (1987) all narrate examples of self-help initiatives in which functions generally provided by the public sector, such as managing public housing projects and caring for public facilities and lands, have been shifted to neighborhood development organizations (NDOs). Fitzgerald (1988) maintains that these examples "signal another trend in the privatization revolution: Neighborhood and community groups are beginning to exercise political clout to extract political concessions and to declare, by steps and degrees, independence from traditional forms of government" (p. 51). He suggests that, as the scarcity of public funds continues, these neighborhood groups—or "shadow governments" (p. 50)—will become an even more visible privatization strategy. In education, self-help includes more moderate activities, such as parents taking their children to school, as well as more radical ideas, such as home schooling.

### User Fees

User Fees—Consumers are charged either a flat or a quantity-related fee for the use of a particular service. (Clarkson, 1989, p. 145)

User fees represent a fifth type of privatization. Also known as "charging" (Bell & Cloke, 1990, p. 9), this strategy, which is housed in Quadrant 2 in Figure 2.1, involves "the imposition of user fees to privately finance public services" (Fixler, 1991, p. 39). Although there is some debate over the issue of whether user fees are a true form of privatization—with some scholars arguing that charging is not a form of privatization and others asserting that it is a type of "quasi-privatization" (Fixler, 1991, p. 39) or a "kind of creeping privatization" (Kolderie, 1991, p. 258)—the majority feel that this vehicle is a viable form of privatization:

> It may be argued that a user charge is antithetical to the basic idea of privatization, for it is merely another method for collecting funds to be expended by government. This is faulty and shortsighted reasoning. A service financed by a user charge should be compared to a service financed by taxes, both of which are provided by the same delivery arrangement. The cost of the latter is obscured, but the cost of the former is highly visible. If hidden subsidies for government-produced services are prohibited, and the full cost of service is charged to the user, citizens will start looking for alternatives if they feel the service is not worth the price. (Savas, 1987, pp. 248-249)

As noted above, "user fees are designed to foster financing of public services by the direct beneficiaries" (Clarkson, 1989, p. 149) rather than by the taxpayers in general (President's Commission on Privatization, 1988). One purpose of user fees is to raise funds. However, the primary objective of "linking spending programs directly to taxes levied for that purpose" (Savas, 1987, p. 248) is to "satisfy people's demands more cost effectively" (p. 249) by "reveal[ing] the true cost of the service" (p. 248). Currently, user fees are an underutilized form of privatization (Clarkson, 1989), although it is likely that the imposition of such charges will increase (Savas, 1987). User fees in education are rare, but examples can be found in the levying of charges for cocurricular activities and certain science laboratory classes.

### Contracting

> The most common method, and the one that people usually mean when they speak of privatization, is contracting out. Under this arrangement, governments purchase services from

the private sector, either from for-profit or not-for-profit organizations. (Savas, 1985, p. 18)

"Privatization" by contract is an operational notion of privatization—in which a traditional responsibility of government is maintained but conducted by a private firm —and yet the *état* power of government is responsible for both the policy and the financial success of the "private" actor. (Bailey, 1987, p. 140)

Contracting and the other privatization strategies in Quadrant 3 of Figure 2.1, "by shifting only the locus of service production ... privatize the means of policy implementation but not the functional sphere of government action" (Starr, 1987, p. 125). Privatization in Quadrant 3 means "retaining collective financing but delegating delivery to the private sector" (Donahue, 1989, p. 215): "The public sector remains the financer, but not the producer" (Pack, 1991, p. 296). Throughout this volume, I demonstrate that the use of private firms to deliver public services involves not only a shift in the balance of public and private goods and services but also a "blurring of the public-private boundary" (Starr, 1991, p. 30). I also reveal that most of the privatization that is occurring and being advocated in the United States is captured by the strategies listed in Quadrant 3, especially the strategy that is central to this volume, contracting.

Contracting is the "best known" (Clarkson, 1989, p. 169), the "most extensive" (Pack, 1991, p. 304), the "most convenient" (Gormley, 1991b, p. 312), the "most popular" (De Hoog, 1984, p. 5), and the "most commonly promoted" (Fitzgerald et al., 1990, p. 71) form of privatization in the United States. Its attractiveness arises from a number of factors. To begin with, given the limited nationalization of industry that has occurred in this country, the use of the more radical measures popular in other countries, such as asset sales and load shedding, are restricted (Pack, 1991). The popularity of contracting also "stems in part from the existence of legislative guidelines for the procurement of goods and the management of contracts, and from the degree of control that a governing body may retain over a service" (Clarkson, 1989, p. 169). Finally, whereas most Americans are eager to secure greater efficiency in the production of goods and services in the public sector, considerably fewer are willing to overturn the welfare state completely (Gormley, 1991a). Stated alternatively, for most government services, the issue of allocative efficiency is subordinated to the issue of technical efficiency (Pack, 1991). Contracting out is particularly useful in this context, for it maintains a central role for the government in helping to define and finance services for its citizens while it holds out the possibility that those services can be produced more efficiently.

As with all strategies in Quadrant 3, contracting out rests on the assumption that "few theoretical differences exist between public and private sector goods and services in how they can be supplied" (De Hoog, 1984, p. 5). It also draws strength from claims that "production is not the government's strong suit" (Savas, 1987, p. 288)—that "privatization by prudent contracting permits government to continue providing a service but to limit itself to the roles that best suit it: articulating the demand, acting as purchasing agent, monitoring the contractor's performance, and paying the bill" (p. 288). Through this arrangement, a variety of desirable outcomes—cost savings, flexibility, and responsiveness—are expected.

The topic of "the variations of contracting for services also deserves some attention" (Kolderie & Hauer, 1991, p. 87). To begin with, there can be significant variation in the number and types of contractors employed (Clarkson, 1989). Government agencies can contract with an assortment of producers, including private firms, nonprofit organizations, voluntary or neighborhood groups, or their own in-house departments (Savas, 1987; Worsnop, 1992). They can also split production among these different sectors (Dudek & Company, 1989; Worsnop, 1992). As we noted earlier, patterns by type of producer often characterize the privatization of different areas of government operations. For example, for-profit private firms tend to be associated with utility services, whereas in health and human services, contracts with nonprofit organizations and neighborhood groups are most prevalent (Clarkson, 1989). There are also variations in the level of the production cycle, with "contracting . . . used most often for the procurement of intermediate goods" (Pack, 1991, p. 283), but with increasing frequency for inputs and final services as well.

Variations also exist because the different domains of production —policy, administration, and service provision (Ismael, 1988)—can be highlighted in contracting. Or, to use Hirsch's (1991) terminology, different patterns of "vertical disintegration" (p. 27) can be realized.

According to Hirsch, vertical disintegration occurs when a government agency that previously maintained control over all domains
contracts out one or more of these activities to a nonpublic agency.
This "vertical disintegration can take place in different parts of the
vertical supply chain" (p. 27). For example, policy oversight and
provision of a given service area may be retained in the public sphere,
whereas management may be contracted to a private firm (President's Commission on Privatization, 1988):

> There are instances when government enters into a contract
> with a private management company to manage a public
> enterprise. For example, some municipalities contract out to
> private firms the managing of a municipal bus service or
> other types of urban transportation. Government then owns
> all the physical assets, the employees are public employees,
> and the government collects the fare from commuters—but
> the management service is provided by a private firm. (Hirsch,
> 1991, p. 32)

Alternatively, policy oversight and administration can be maintained in the public sphere while a government unit contracts with a
nonpublic agency to assume responsibility for production.

Another reason for variations in contracting springs from the fact
that there is considerable diversity in the ways service delivery is
treated by government agencies. They

> can purchase a service, or they can break the service down
> into its different components and buy certain elements of it:
> pieces of the work itself, support services for the work, the
> supervision of the work or of the support services, or the
> equipment and facilities needed for the work. (Kolderie &
> Hauer, 1991, p. 87)

For example, some or all of the support functions (e.g., transportation, maintenance, housekeeping) of public agencies in areas such as
corrections and education can be contracted out. On the other hand,
the core service itself (i.e., custodial care in corrections and teaching
in education) can be handed over to private producers.

Finally, there is considerable variance in two other aspects of
contracting—contractor selection and type of contract developed—

that merit acknowledgment. The most common methods used to select a contractor at the local government level are as follows: lowest bid among qualified companies (57.5%), other (23.9%), lowest bid (12.3%), and best reputation (6.3%). The data on types of contracts that local agencies employ with contractors, in turn, are as follows: firm fixed price (43.4%), fixed price with incentives (25.9%), fixed price with escalation (14.6%), cost plus incentive fee (2.2%), fixed price with incentive (1.6%), and cost plus fixed fee (1.6%) (Roehm, Castellano, & Karns, 1991).

There are numerous examples of contracting in education. Historically, contracting has focused on support services. More recently, however, examples of contracting that address the core functions of schooling have begun to surface.

### Franchises

Franchising is a privatization method whereby government grants a private entity (or entities) authority to provide a particular service within a specific geographical area. (Clarkson, 1989, p. 146)

With franchising, as with all the privatization strands in Quadrant 3 of Figure 2.1, "government is the arranger and a private organization is the producer of the service" (Savas, 1987, p. 75). Thus, franchising shares a good deal in common with contracting. They "can be distinguished[, however,] by the means of payment to the producer" (p. 75). Under contracting, the government assumes responsibility for compensating the producer. With franchises, "users pay the service providers directly" (Peters, 1991, p. 55). Although there is considerable variability in the extent of government responsibilities in franchises—"from nominal, where private service-providers are licensed without controls on price or quality, to a very extensive role, where conditions of the franchise may include health, safety, price, quality and service-level requirements" (Clarkson, 1989, p. 146)—the primary role is regulatory (Clarkson, 1989; Peters, 1991).

Hanke and Walters (1987) have identified two basic forms of franchises—those in which "the expenses for the installation of major civil works are borne by the local community" (p. 111) and those in which "a private company is entrusted with construction of the facility as well as its operation" (p. 110), what Scully and Cole (1991) call a full-service franchise. For a variety of reasons, including the increasing difficulty that government agencies are experiencing in raising capital funds and favorable changes in the tax laws, this second type of franchise—"the provision of 'full services' on a 'turn-key' basis" (Fixler & Poole, 1991, p. 75) or "lease-back arrangement" (Committee on the Judiciary, 1986, p. 137)—is growing in popularity (Fixler & Poole, 1991; Seader, 1991). At the same time, it is important to note that because franchising "can only be employed for services received by the identifiable individuals since the provider must charge consumers directly" (Peters, 1991, p. 55), this privatization strategy has not been used extensively. Exclusive contracts to provide class rings or caps and gowns to prospective high school graduates are examples of franchises in education.

### Vouchers

> Another form of privatization is the voucher, whereby certain consumers are authorized to purchase earmarked goods or services from the private market. The government specifies who is eligible to purchase the services and who is eligible to provide them. (Gormley, 1991a, p. 4)

"The use of vouchers keeps financing in the public sector" (Pack, 1991, p. 283) while "distributing purchasing power to eligible consumers" (President's Commission on Privatization, 1988, p. 2). A system of vouchers is "designed to encourage the consumption of particular goods by a particular class of consumers" (Savas, 1987, p. 78). Under a voucher program, anyone "issued a voucher can use it as a form of currency or scrip to purchase supplies, goods, or services in the open market" (Savas, 1985, p. 19). In moving production responsibility from the government to the private sector via "subsidies to consumers" (Peters, 1991, p. 56), vouchers "initiate a much more rigorous form of competition than competitive bidding" (Gormley, 1991b, p. 313) or contracting. In some real sense, by permitting "consumers to exercise relatively free choice in the market place" (Savas, 1987, p. 78), a voucher system "resembles a free market" (Peters, 1991, p. 55).

Vouchers are particularly useful in allowing "markets to continue to operate with minimal government involvement while catering to low-income segments of the population" (Butler, 1991, p. 23).

In addition to other benefits, it is argued that "redistributional goals or externalities are more efficiently reached by vouchers" (Pack, 1991, pp. 283-284), that "monitoring and quality control of services" (Clarkson, 1989, p. 147) are enhanced, and that the growth of public spending coalitions is stunted (Butler, 1987). Although well-known examples of voucher systems are in place in the United States—such as the food stamp program and the GI bill—and other uses—such as for K-12 education and housing—have long been suggested (Savas, 1985), vouchers are an infrequently used privatization strategy (Clarkson, 1989; Peters, 1991). The recent Milwaukee initiative to provide funds to low-income parents to send their children to schools of their choice is an example of a voucher program in education.

### Grants /Subsidies

The use of grants and subsidies is another method for foster-ing the privatization of public services. Under this approach, government provides financial or in-kind contributions to private organizations or individuals to encourage them to provide a service. (Clarkson, 1989, p. 146)

The use of the term *subsidies* in this book refers to the "general strategy of changing the demand for public-sector goods by altering the incentive structure and thus creating self-interest coalitions" (Butler, 1987, p. 12). The goal is "to make the private sector more responsive to public goals through a manipulation of incentives thought to govern market behavior" (Hula, 1990b, p. 7). Or, stated more concretely, the objective of subsidies is "to encourage private organizations to provide a service" (Peters, 1991, p. 55) "at reduced costs to users" (Clarkson, 1989, p. 170). As such, "subsidies shift expected returns of alternative economic decisions in favor of those supported by public authorities" (Hula, 1990b, p. 7). A variety of measures find a home under this broad construct, including direct cash payments; in-kind contributions; use of materials, equipment, land, and facilities; low-cost loans; and tax abatement and other taxing powers, such as modified depreciation rules (Clarkson, 1989; Hula, 1990b; Savas, 1987). A tax program that encourages corpora-tions to donate materials, supplies, and equipment to schools is a good example of privatization via a subsidy.

## Deregulation

> Also considered privatization, deregulation of industry has been one of the most important forms of curbing government and relying more heavily on the private sector. (President's Commission on Privatization, 1988, p. 2)

I reported above that, unlike many other countries, the United States has not nationalized much of its industry. Alternatively, the United States has relied extensively on widespread government regulation of private sector industries. Thus, "the widespread deregulation movement in the United States has been a home-grown version of what in other nations has taken the form of outright divestiture of government properties" (President's Commission on Privatization, 1988, p. 229). Although theoretically distinct from privatization, this process of opening an industry to competitive pressures—known as liberalization (Starr, 1987; Vickers & Yarrow, 1988)—is often tightly linked with the transfer of the allocation and/or provision of services out of the public sector.

At the heart of the deregulation movement is an attempt to privatize "many so-called public services . . . through the free market" (Savas, 1985, p. 21). As with subsidies, the goal is to foster the private provision of activities historically housed in the public sector (Fixler & Poole, 1991). Along with franchises, deregulation is viewed as a particularly robust form of privatization (Butler, 1991). It works by "expanding the role of the marketplace" (Savas, 1987, p. 240)—by "encouraging private-sector providers to bid for the consumer's attention" (Butler, 1987, p. 12)—thus "increas[ing] the number of providers competing to supply a given service" (Clarkson, 1989, p. 149). "This removal or weakening of various legislative controls" (Bell & Cloke, 1990, p. 9) is generally accomplished by "the repealing of an existing monopoly held by public enterprise" (Hirsch, 1991, p. 28), "the relaxation of entry controls" (Bell & Cloke, 1990, p. 9), and "the reduction of exit barriers" (Hirsch, 1991, p. 28). The recent debate at the state level in Pennsylvania to change code language to allow districts to purchase teaching and management services from outside sources is a good example of deregulation in education (McLaughlin, 1995).

## Conclusion

This chapter continued preparing the scaffolding upon which a deeper understanding of privatization can be constructed. I started that work by providing a definition of privatization and then reviewing the objectives that privatization is designed to meet. Finally, based on the dimensions of the allocation and provision of services, I presented a typology of 10 privatization strategies.

In the United States, privatization means primarily "enlisting private energies to improve the performance of tasks that [should] remain in some sense public" (Donahue, 1989, p. 7). Therefore, although the focus on privatization in this volume is comprehensive, the spotlight shines most brightly on the perspectives found in Quadrant 3 of Figure 2.1. Of those, three have particular relevance for education: contracting, vouchers, and deregulation. Given that two of these strands—vouchers and deregulation—have already received considerable attention in the education literature, our discussion throughout this volume, while attending to the larger agenda of publicly financed services provided by the nonpublic sector, also highlights the topic of contracting.

The remainder of this book completes the groundwork needed to better understand privatization in education. I turn next to an analysis of the historical context of privatization.

# THE HISTORICAL CONTEXT OF PRIVATIZATION | 3

The frontiers of public and private responsibilities are not easily located, and nor are they constant. (Martin, 1993, p. 189)

The current trend towards privatisation and deregulation was mirrored in the past by nationalisation and regulation, particularly in the immediate post-war period, and it is not improbable that the pendulum may swing back. (Bell & Cloke, 1990, p. 3)

This chapter traces the evolution of privatization as a policy initiative. The first part examines the growth of the public sector between 1900 and 1980. Data are presented to illustrate this phenomenon. The focus then shifts to the rationale for that expansion. The second half of the chapter addresses the expansion of privatization. Here, we review the roots of the current privatization movement and examine the extent of privatization in the United States over the past 25 years.

## Development of the Public Sector

The growth of public sectors [is] an expression of the economic and industrial reality of its time. (Martin, 1993, p. 20)

The colonial city had very few governmental functions. . . .
[It] could maintain the peace, adjudicate disputes, own and
manage property, sue and be sued, and own and manage
municipal enterprises, but throughout the colonial period
city government "had not too much to do" and spent very
little. The escalating pace and impact of nineteenth century
urbanization, industrialization, and massive immigration
generated conditions, however, that overwhelmed municipalities. (Fitzgerald et al., 1990, p. 69)

### Growth of the Public Sector

When speaking of . . . government [growth], individuals
may be referring to many different characteristics of the
public sector, including the burden of taxes to support the
public sector, the regulatory burden of government, the size
of the public budget, the number of public sector employees,
and the number of government programs and agencies.
(Berry & Lowery, 1987, p. 15)

The role of government, its size, and its expenditures have
been expanding—conservatives might say exploding—for
forty years. (Hirsch, 1991, p. 9)

At the outset of World War I, the role of government at all levels
in the United States was quite limited (Elkin, 1987): "The federal
government engaged in only a narrow range of activities [and]
imposed essentially no taxes other than the tariff" (Worsnop, 1992,
p. 986). State responsibilities were similarly narrow and, although
local governments carried out a wider array of activities, they too
were very limited by present-day norms (Worsnop, 1992): "The
number of municipal- and state-performed business activities was
only a small percentage of the total economy" (Hanke, 1987, p. 1).
From these humble beginnings, government and its services have
expanded dramatically over the course of the century, particularly
in the period following World War II. For example, "at the turn of
the century, when government employment was 4 percent of the
total labor force, the tax share was 8 percent of output. In 1929,
respective figures were 6 percent and 11 percent, in 1974, 15 percent

and 32 percent" (Meltzer & Scott, 1978, p. 113). By 1980, the government was employing nearly one in five (18.8%) people (Rose, 1984)—a figure that has remained relatively constant over the past dozen years (Tax Foundation, 1993). In absolute terms, government expenditures increased four hundred-fold from the turn of the century to the mid-1970s. In terms of constant dollars, the growth rate was ninety-four-fold. Controlling for population growth (i.e., reporting on a per capita basis), we see a twenty-eight-fold growth rate in the public sector during the first three quarters of the 20th century (Musgrave & Musgrave, 1976, p. 132).

> In about fifty years, government expenditures have grown a hundredfold, from an eighth to more than a third of the gross national product (GNP). Even when adjusted by subtracting expenditures for national defense, foreign aid, and veterans' benefits, the growth pattern persists. Per capita expenditures, adjusted in this manner and expressed in constant dollars, have increased more than sevenfold during this period. (Savas, 1987, p. 14)

> Inflation, population growth, and an increase in defense-related expenditures account for much of the absolute growth of government, but the real growth was large even after allowing for these effects. (Savas, 1982, p. 12)

Federal-level expenditures (including indirect expenditures) have expanded in dramatic fashion, increasing from 19% of civil expenditures in 1902 to 44% in 1984 (Aronson & Hilley, 1986; Maxwell & Aronson, 1977; Ross, 1988).

As the Musgraves (1976) remind us, a particularly useful way to assess the growth of the public sector is "to focus . . . on the share of government in total expenditures" (p. 132). Using this measure, we see that total government expenditures in the United States have been as follows: 7% of GNP in 1902; 10% in 1929; 23% in 1950; 32% in 1970 and 1979; and 35% in 1987 and 1992 (Mueller, 1989; Musgrave & Musgrave, 1976; Shannon, 1981; Tax Foundation, 1993)—a fivefold increase in the relative size of the public sector (Musgrave & Musgrave, 1976). Or, "relative to the size of the economy, the government has increased in size by more than 80 percent over the postwar era" (Berry & Lowery, 1987, p. 17). Tables 3.1 and 3.2 reveal

TABLE 3.1   Government Employment

| Year | Number of employees (millions)[a] | As percentage of population | As percentage of all employees[b] |
|------|------|------|------|
| 1929 | 2.92 | 2.4 | 7.9 |
| 1939 | 5.79 | 4.4 | 16.0 |
| 1950 | 5.69 | 3.8 | 11.0 |
| 1960 | 7.89 | 4.4 | 13.1 |
| 1970 | 11.35 | 5.6 | 15.1 |
| 1980 | 14.12 | 6.2 | 14.7 |
| 1983 | 13.86 | 5.9 | 14.2 |

SOURCE: Savas (1987, p. 17). Reprinted by permission.
a. Full-time equivalents, excluding military.
b. Includes only nonagricultural civilian workers.

the extent of government growth in terms of two other indicators—
employment and expenditures.

### Explaining the Growth of Government Services

The need to understand why government grows so rapidly
seems urgent. (Buchanan, 1977, p. 3)

In reviewing the hypothesized causes for the size and growth
of government, one is essentially also reviewing the explanations for the existence of government. (Mueller, 1989,
p. 323)

To search for the cause of big government in a single conscious choice in the past or present is to misunderstand the
historical process. . . . In fact, the size of government reflects
the interaction of conscious choices, unanticipated events,
and long-term political, social, and economic processes.
(Rose, 1984, pp. 31-32)

Economists and political scientists have employed a variety of
frameworks to explain the rising pattern of public expenditures over
the past 75 years. I outline the most important of their theories[1] here
under the following 10 headings: reaction to corruption; growing

**TABLE 3.2** Federal, State, and Local Expenditures

| (1) Year | (2) Total (billions) | (3) As percentage of GNP | (4) Total, excluding national defense and veteran expenditures (billions) | (5) (4) as percentage of GNP | (6) (4) in constant 1967 dollars (billions) | (7) (4) as per capita expenditures in constant 1967 dollars |
|---|---|---|---|---|---|---|
| 1930 | $ 11.1 | 12.2 | $ 9.6 | 10.6 | $ 23.9 | $ 194 |
| 1940 | 18.4 | 18.4 | 16.3 | 16.3 | 44.4 | 336 |
| 1950 | 61.0 | 21.3 | 41.4 | 14.5 | 61.1 | 404 |
| 1960 | 136.4 | 27.0 | 83.7 | 16.5 | 96.3 | 537 |
| 1970 | 313.4 | 31.6 | 223.7 | 22.5 | 193.4 | 951 |
| 1980 | 869.0 | 33.1 | 707.0 | 26.9 | 313.3 | 1,383 |
| 1983 | 1,167.5 | 35.3 | 922.8 | 27.9 | 338.8 | 1,445 |

SOURCE: Savas (1987, p. 15). Reprinted by permission.

visibility of market imperfections; increased significance of income redistribution; additional demands for public services; revenue growth; growth through crisis; costs of public services; the presence of spending coalitions; fiscal illusion; and the pull of existing programs. I follow Rose (1984) in assuming that a variety of influences working in tandem best explains the growth in the size of government.

*Reaction to Corruption*

As Bell and Cloke (1990) have noted, the growth of the public sector during much of the 1900s is, to some extent, the result of a longer term cyclical tug of war between private and public provision of services. In short, the growth spurt of the 1900s is in some ways a reaction to the conditions prevalent during the last part of the 19th century, especially (a) to "the social Darwinism and the laissez-faire theories that were prevalent" (President's Commission on Privatization, 1988, p. 230), a sort of "natural rights/limited government philosophy" (Fixler, 1991, p. 44); (b) to the "discontent with the vast social changes caused by industrialization after the Civil War" (Worsnop, 1992, p. 986); (c) to the corruption and economic avarice of the era—to the "cronyism . . . and other forms of corruption" (Darr, 1991, p. 61) in existing contracting initiatives, to the perceived corruption of machine bosses (Fitzgerald et al., 1990), and to the rampant abuses of private sector industries; and (d) "to the great political and economic power being newly exercised by large, concentrated industries" (President's Commission on Privatization, 1988, p. 227). Thus, one root of public sector expansion was the Progressive movement with its prevailing belief that providing services publicly would overcome the "so-called spoils system" (Borcherding, 1977b, p. 61), "reduce opportunities for graft and mismanagement" (Gomez-Ibanez, Meyer, & Luberoff, 1990, p. 148), and "check excessive corporate power" (President's Commission on Privatization, 1988, p. 227). It was from this movement that the "contemporary programmes of the welfare state" took root—a growth process that did not reach full maturity until the 1960s and 1970s (Rose, 1984, p. 32).

*Growing Visibility of Market Imperfections*

Implicit in each justification for political action is the view that government offers a corrective alternative to the market. . . . The most common justification for political action is an alleged failure of the market system to produce a set of goods which a significant proportion of the population wants produced. These are typically public goods whose benefits once produced can not be restricted to those who pay for them. (Hula, 1990b, p. 6)

The classic economic argument for the presence of government goods and services centers on the issue of social goods and market failure (Mueller, 1989; Musgrave & Musgrave, 1976; Peirce, 1981). Specifically, the market can function only "where the 'exclusion principle' applies, i.e., when A's consumption is made contingent on his paying the price while B, who does not pay, is excluded" (Musgrave & Musgrave, 1976, p. 50). However, when consumption is nonrival and/or if exclusion is not possible, then a "political process of budget determination becomes necessary" (p. 51).

These characteristics of pure public goods have given rise to a recognition that, if some pure public goods are going to be provided, the coercive capacity of the state must be employed to raise the revenues required to cover the costs of their provision. (Wilson, 1990, p. 60)

A second justification for government activity in this area revolves around the issue of "market imperfections" (Hula, 1990b, p. 6). These include situations "that arise in industries where competition is impossible or undesirable" (Vickers & Yarrow, 1988, p. 45). Public action is also required to deal with "external economies or diseconomies" (Pack, 1991, p. 282), or the spillover effects of market activities (Musgrave & Musgrave, 1976; Renner, 1989)—for example, the social, as opposed to private, benefits of education or the social costs of pollution. A final market imperfection providing legitimacy to government activity is "the lack of necessary information on the part of consumers" (President's Commission on Privatization, 1988, p. 236).

For our purposes here, the important issue is that, as society has become more complex, market failures and imperfections have become more common, more visible, and more unacceptable. In particular, more goods and services reflect the qualities of nonrivalness and nonexclusiveness. Perhaps even more significant, spillover effects are more pronounced today than they were a century ago. Coming at the issue from a slightly different angle, it can be argued that the number of collective goods has grown in recent times (Savas, 1987)—or, more appropriately, that "certain designated private and toll goods . . . have migrated into the class of collective goods" (Savas, 1987, p. 53). For example:

> Not long ago education was regarded as a private good. . . . In time, however, a new understanding gained ground: The entire society benefited significantly if everyone was educated, much like vaccination. Education was considered to have major, positive side effects associated with it, and therefore it was not only made freely available to all, but its consumption was actually made compulsory, up to a certain age or grade level. (Savas, 1987, p. 53)

Such a pattern leads, of course, to considerable expansion of the public sector.

The largest cause of government growth is the "societal decision that certain private and toll goods, such as food, education, and mass transit, are so worthy that their consumption should be encouraged regardless of the consumer's ability to pay" (Savas, 1987, p. 52). Indeed, after factoring out interest on debt and defense spending, these predominantly private and toll goods now account for two thirds of federal expenditures and roughly three fifths of state and local expenditures (Savas, 1987, pp. 55-56).

*Increased Significance*
*of Income Redistribution*

An important rationale for public sector activity centers on the distribution function of government (Mueller, 1989; Oates, 1972), specifically "adjustment of the distribution of income and wealth to assure conformance with what society considers a 'fair' or 'just' state of distribution" (Musgrave & Musgrave, 1976, p. 6). The reasoning here is that even when the market works, its outcomes may be unacceptable (Hula, 1990b).

As was true in our above analysis of social goods, definitions of acceptable and unacceptable market outcomes in the area of income distribution have changed rather dramatically from 1900 to 1975. This change, in turn, has given rise to enhanced government activity in the redistribution of income, especially to ameliorate social ills (Phares, 1981) through the provision of "socially necessary services" (Walters, 1987, p. 83):

> Growth of government is fueled by a belief in greater equality of condition. When we also observe that movements to decrease social distinctions . . . aim to achieve equality of condition, the growth of public spending is clearly part and parcel of the movement toward equality of condition. As long as this value increases in importance, and as long as government is viewed as an agent of redistribution of resources, government spending will continue to grow. . . . The greater the preference for equality, the larger the growth of government. (Wildavsky, 1985, pp. 61, 70)

Demographic changes that have increased the number of citizens eligible for these social benefits have compounded the growth of government services (Rose, 1984). For example, when social security benefits were introduced, payments started later than the life expectancy age (by 18 years in Great Britain) (Rose, 1984). Today, because of demographic changes, payouts begin considerably before the average life expectancy age (by 9 years for men in the United States, for example).

Indeed, there is considerable evidence of the growth of social welfare spending in this country since the Depression (American Enterprise Institute, 1970; Elkin, 1987). Musgrave and Musgrave (1976) document that "the most striking feature" (p. 137) in the changing pattern of civilian expenditures during the first three quarters of the 20th century "is the rising share of social welfare expenditures" (pp. 137-138). In particular, "the postwar increase in public expenditures at all levels of government, as well as the shift toward an increasing federal share has been largely due to increased social welfare expenditure" (Bahl, 1984, p. 12). As a percentage of GNP, social welfare spending increased from 4.4% in 1954 to 15.9% in 1980 (Bahl, 1984). As a percentage of gross domestic product (GDP), social welfare spending jumped from 10.4% in 1960 to 18.5% in 1989 (Tax Foundation, 1993).

*Additional Demands for Public Services*

Implicit in what we reported above is the simple reality that public services have grown during much of this century because demand for these services is increasing:

> Without doubt, some considerable part of the observed growth in the public sector, at all levels, is directly traceable to the demands of the citizenry, genuine demands for more services accompanied by an increased willingness to shoulder the tax burden required for financing. (Buchanan, 1977, p. 6)

Two additional factors—income growth and industrialization—have added to the demand for a larger government sector of the economy. In economic theory, "Wagner's law asserts that, as the level of per capita income in society increases, public expenditures will increase even more than proportionately" (Oates, 1972, p. 200)— "that the efficient product mix between private and social goods changes as per capita income rises, and that this change involves a rising share of social goods" (Musgrave & Musgrave, 1976, p. 140). The evidence here is somewhat consistent with Wagner's assertion (Oates, 1972; Rose, 1984).

Next to the income rationale, "the most frequently used and accepted explanation for the growth of government is that it is caused by increasing . . . industrialization" (Wildavsky, 1985, p. 60). This is the case because industrialization promotes urbanization and accompanying "societal interdependencies" (Berry & Lowery, 1987, p. 52), which "are not well handled by private markets" (Borcherding, 1977b, p. 52). Considerable pressure to expand public services results:

> As urbanization increases, people get in each other's way. More police officers are needed. New kinds of government action are called for to regulate and ameliorate harmful and potentially harmful side effects of individual actions—for instance, to monitor and control air and water pollution; to reduce noise; to investigate foods, drugs, and restaurants; to segregate certain activities by zoning. All these have required government expenditures. (Savas, 1982, p. 12)

Industrialization also leads to greater complexity "and to a vast increase in the range and scale of so-called public infrastructure and services" (Hanke, 1985, p. 3). Technological advances associated with industrial growth accompanied by demands for capital that outstrip the capacity of the private sector also foster government intervention (Berry & Lowery, 1987). Industrialization has also helped ratchet up the standards for minimal levels of acceptable services in a variety of domains (Fitzgerald et al., 1990; Hirsch, 1991). It also ensures that citizens are "better placed to make their demands effective politically" (Rose, 1984, p. 40), thus expanding demand for services already in the public sphere as well as providing an impetus for government to tackle the wide assortment of problems that accompany industrialization (Savas, 1982, 1987).

## Revenue Growth

According to this theory, growth of the public sector can be traced to the expanding supply of revenue available to the government, what Rose (1984) refers to as "buoyant revenue" (p. 37) and what is generally known in the field of economics as the "fiscal dividend" (Musgrave & Musgrave, 1976, p. 558). Berry and Lowery (1987) concentrate on one part of the fiscal dividend—the increasing efficiencies by which tax revenues are being collected. They describe "a number of changes that have taken place in the U.S. economy in the postwar period . . . involving the integration of workers employed outside the taxable-wage system of employment into that system" (p. 54). In particular, they theorize that shifts away from occupations where tax collection is difficult—that is, where income can be hidden or where bartering is common—have raised the supply of revenue. Similarly, they maintain that the movement from noncorporate to corporate firm arrangements since the war has helped generate more tax revenue "because of the greater stringency of corporate income reporting requirements" (p. 54). According to this aspect of the fiscal dividend theory, important changes in the fabric of labor and business markets have created a number of new "tax handles" (Musgrave & Musgrave, 1976, p. 145) and "reaped a windfall of new revenue" (Berry & Lowery, 1987, p. 54) for the government, a windfall that is being devoted largely to the growth of the public sector (Buchanan, 1977).

Another, and generally better known, dimension of the fiscal dividend theory highlights other "technical features of the revenue system" (Rose, 1984, p. 37), specifically "the built-in gain in revenue" (Musgrave & Musgrave, 1976, p. 559) that materializes because the economy is generally expanding (Buchanan, 1977), because taxes are not generally levied in fixed sums but as percentages of sales or income, and because of inflation (Bennett & Johnson, 1980). Progressive taxes in periods of growth promote even faster revenue accumulation (Rose, 1984). Fiscal dividend theory holds that "legislators, whether in the Congress or in the state assemblies . . . treat this automatic revenue increase as free money to be used for new spending programs" (Buchanan, 1977, p. 12).

*Growth Through Crisis*

This rationale, better known as the "threshold theory" (Musgrave & Musgrave, 1976, p. 146), the "displacement theory" (Rose, 1984, p. 52), or the "concentration-displacement explanation" (Berry & Lowery, 1987, p. 56), posits that political shocks or crises raise the level of government growth in noticeable increments. According to the theory, during periods of crisis "people's thresholds of tax tolerance permanently rise" (Borcherding, 1977a, p. 37): "Crises are expected to alter the public's expectations about the appropriate size of government so that the public sector grows in a ratchetlike manner" (Berry & Lowery, 1987, p. 74). When a political shock passes, revenue will fall, but not to precrisis levels. In effect, the additional resources "will be displaced in other programmes" (Rose, 1984, p. 52) "by expansion-minded politicians and bureaucrats" (Borcherding, 1977a, p. 38). "The supply of revenue [thus] sustains a level of programmes far above what would have been possible" (Rose, 1984, p. 58) in the absence of the intervening crises. The Great Depression and World War II are often cited as examples of political crises sufficient to trigger displacement effects.

*Costs of Public Services*

Analyses of the costs of providing government services contribute still another explanation for public sector growth. For example, Musgrave and Musgrave (1976) reveal that, whereas the overall GNP price index increased by 236% between 1929 and 1974, government expenditures rose by 448% (pp. 142-143). One explanation for this is what Buchanan (1977) labels "the public productivity paradox" (p. 8) and what Rose (1984) refers to as "buoyant costs," the fact that "government costs rise faster than costs in the private sector" (p. 37). Much of this low productivity growth in the public sector—when compared to private sector growth—can be attributed to "greater sensitivity of government purchases to inflation" (Musgrave & Musgrave, 1976, p. 143) and to the fact that the labor-intensive nature of many public services—such as police work and education—make them less likely targets for cost reductions through capital improvements and technological innovations (Bradford, Malt, & Oates, 1969; Mueller, 1989). According to this line of thought, originally developed by Baumol and subsequently labeled the "Baumol effect," the phenomenon of rising taxes with little improvement in the level or quality of public services is due to "the nature of public sector work rather than public sector workers per se" (Berry & Lowery, 1987, p. 103).

Representatives from the public choice school, on the other hand, sketch a less charitable interpretation of the more costly nature of public services (Mueller, 1989; Tullock, 1988). They maintain that the monopoly status enjoyed by many government agencies—and the "information monopoly power" of agency bureaucrats (Berry & Lowery, 1987, p. 8)—create considerable momentum for expanded public sector growth. They also contend that the costs of public services are unreasonably high because monopoly status permits government agencies to overproduce services, overstaff, overpay employees, and overbuild (a bias toward capital spending rather than maintenance) (Ramsey, 1987; Savas, 1982). Thus, "an alternative interpretation of the rising cost of government is that it is caused by government inefficiency" (Rose, 1984, p. 38).

*Presence of Spending Coalitions*

An often-cited cause for the nearly unbroken expansion of the public sector through much of the 20th century is the "inbuilt tendencies toward steady growth and producer domination" (Pirie, 1988, p. 10), that is, to the effect of spending coalitions that work to promote growth through the supply side of the demand-supply equation (Niskanen, 1971)—what Buchanan (1977) labels "the elements of a nondemocratic model of politics" (p. 11) and what Pirie

(1988) characterizes as a "redirection of production factors toward political rather than economic ends" (p. 5). The assumption at the heart of this logic is that "the beneficiaries of government growth support government growth" (Mueller, 1989, p. 332). According to this line of thought, "the public sector has not grown in response to objective needs of the nation, but instead in response to the selfish needs of government itself" (Berry & Lowery, 1987, p. 4):

> Observers have noted the so-called "ratchet" effect, whereby the public sector turns only one way, like an industrial cogwheel designed for that purpose. Big spending governments add new programmes or expand additional ones, and the support of those who benefit locks them into place like the arm which comes down on the cogwheel, making it impossible for them to be reversed. The cumulative effect over the decades has been to increase the size of the public sector year by year. (Pirie, 1988, p. 7)

> The coalition that forms to nurture, protect, and expand a program is comprised of four groups: beneficiaries and near-beneficiaries (the latter are those who expect to become beneficiaries as the program expands); service providers (e.g. construction firms and construction workers engaged in road-building programs); government administrators; and political activists (e.g. officeholders, office seekers, and problem-finding elites). The partners in the coalition interact in almost a choreographed manner to gain gradual increases in spending for their program. (Savas, 1987, p. 30)

According to this line of analysis, "transmission institutions may be deliberately perverted by self-seeking politicians and bureaucrats who succeed in isolating themselves from the discipline inposed by the electoral process" (Buchanan, 1977, p. 11). Thus "two villains often mentioned as instrumental in the growth of government are interest groups and bureaucrats" (Mueller, 1989, p. 333).

To begin with, politicians promote the continual expansion of government services in order to gain the support of voters (Meltzer & Scott, 1978). Because "elected officials gain considerable 'political income' when government grows" (Savas, 1982, p. 17), politicians engage in "tax-funded politics" (Bennett & DiLorenzo, 1987, p. 20)—

or, stated more directly, they "use public money to buy votes" (Savas, 1987, p. 23) "in single-minded pursuit of the goal of election" (Rose, 1984, p. 42). Government administrators, so the argument continues, are so driven by the imperative of budget maximization—with the accompanying power—that they become empire builders, and the bureaucracy itself to a large extent becomes self-generating (Bennett & Johnson, 1980; Borcherding, 1977b; Mueller, 1989; Niskanen, 1971). Because it is also in the self-interest of other government employees to see an expanding public sector, they employ their "coercive voting power" (Berry & Lowery, 1987, p. 41) and political muscle in the service of growth—or "their own interest as producers" (Buchanan, 1977, p. 14)—as well (Bush & Denzau, 1977; Hirsch, 1991). Consumers of government programs with a good deal of interest in preserving their benefits also press for additional spending while actively opposing attempts to rein in expenditures (Berry & Lowery, 1987; Butler, 1987). Finally, service providers in the private sector with a direct or indirect stake in a given public sector (e.g., private defense contractors) assume an advocacy role for additional government spending as well (Butler, 1987).

One result of all of this is that "public sector operations become producer-oriented" (Pirie, 1988, p. 26)—"representative government . . . yields to organized producer interests" (Seldon, 1987, p. 129). A second is that "the political dynamics favor increases in government spending but act strongly against any attempt to reduce outlays. Like a ratchet, the dynamics tend to operate in one direction only— toward growth" (Pirie, 1988, pp. 7-8). Or, as Buchanan (1977) describes it, "the cost-increasing features feed on themselves" (p. 16).

*Fiscal Illusion*

The theory of fiscal illusion rests on emerging knowledge "that alternative tax forms . . . have a potentially powerful effect on the level and composition of public budgets" (Goetz, 1977, p. 186). Central to the theory is the belief that taxpayers use "taxes as prices" (Goetz, 1977, p. 176) to establish a cost-benefit ratio for government services. Building from there, the theory holds that because the revenue structure of taxation masks the true price of taxes, voters "systematically underestimate the costs of public sector goods and services (Berry & Lowery, 1987, p. 43). Costs become illusionary, and citizens are "deceived . . . about the true size of government" (Mueller, 1989, p. 342). It is also suggested in various formulations of the theory that this " 'rational ignorance' on the part of voters" (Berry & Lowery, 1987, p. 43), although sometimes chosen by taxpayers (Buchanan, 1977), is often manipulated by political elites who deliberately distort preferences for public expenditures in the service of their own political ambitions (Berry & Lowery, 1987; Mueller, 1989).

*Pull of Existing Programs*

According to this line of analysis, size begets growth. One formulation of this phenomenon has been framed by Rose (1984), who maintains that "in politics inertia refers to the tendency of a body in motion to continue in motion" (p. 49). A second has been captured by Wildavsky (cited in Rose, 1984) in the maxim that "political addition is easier than political subtraction" (p. 50). The size-promotes-growth argument rests on a variety of well-anchored footings. To begin with, scholars in this area point out that history exercises considerable influence over the future, especially when funding is at stake. Decisions made in the past tend to ossify, making change difficult at best. As Rose (1984) notes, government programs become increasingly difficult to alter because they become "constrained by a fine mesh of commitments spun around [them] through the years" (p. 49).

Added to these dynamics is the political reality that the large organizational and legal infrastructure put in place to manage the public sector has "far greater persistence than politicians holding office at the will of the electorate" (Rose, 1984, p. 49). Scholars contend that the system itself, as it expands, continually reduces the degrees of freedom that would allow reformers to capitalize on periodic calls for reduction of public sector services. Also fueling the forces for growth is the increasingly interlocking nature of public programs: "The more programmes that government adopts, the greater the probability that one programme will affect another" (p. 50). The result is a continual spiral upward as action in one place in the interconnected system creates demand for additional efforts in other sectors.

## The Development of the
## Modern Privatization Movement

If major institutional changes could be made, government budgets could be slashed (along with taxes) without reducing the quantity or quality of goods and services enjoyed by the final consumer, the taxpaying citizen. But a shift in approach would be required to accomplish this. *Government financing of goods and services must be divorced from direct government provision or production of these goods and services.* . . . Through the simple device of introducing private provision under government financing, the growth in government spending may, figuratively speaking, be stopped in its tracks. (Buchanan, 1977, p. 17)

Looking back, the year 1979 may well be seen as a high-water mark in the growth of state economic power. What had seemed until then as perhaps an inevitable and remorseless growth of the public sector has been sent into sharp reverse. (Pirie, 1988, pp. 14-15)

### Privatization in Historical Context

Privatization is even older than government. Its origins are lost in antiquity. (Savas, 1985, p. 17)

#### Early Origins

Although privatization is a relatively new term, "making no significant appearance in political or economic literature before 1979" (Pirie, 1988, p. 3), "the various activities that have been described as privatization can claim a longer history" (Hemming & Mansoor, 1988, p. 1): "Private organizations have been involved in public undertakings throughout history" (Donahue, 1989, p. 34):

Privatization is quite old. One need only think of the Hessians to see an example of contracting out from about two hundred years ago. Mercenaries were a veritable private industry in the time of classical Greece, and contract management of cities was a fact of life in Renaissance Italy. (Florestano, 1991, p. 292)

> And let us remember that it was a private contractor, en-
> gaged by Spanish monarchs, who set foot in the New World
> in 1492. (Savas, 1987, p. 69)

In the United States, at the federal level, the government "has been
contracting out services and selling assets since the early years of the
Republic" (Starr, 1991, p. 26):

> Privatization . . . can be traced to the first Bank of the United
> States which served as the federal government's fiscal
> agency and principal depository of the treasury and was
> owned by private shareholders. When the federal govern-
> ment wanted to deliver mail to its citizens west of the Mis-
> sissippi, it contracted with 80 horseback riders and spawned
> the Pony Express. The Homestead Act gave settlers govern-
> ment-owned land for a small fee if they would cultivate soil
> for a fixed period. (Miller & Tufts, 1991, p. 99)

> Prior to the nineteenth century even such essential activities
> of government as the collection of taxes and the organization
> of military units were often performed by profit-seeking
> organizations. (Niskanen, 1971, p. 19)

At the state level, private contractors have been assuming responsibilities for prisoners for over a century (Committee on the Judiciary,
1986). And at the local level, "transportation and fire protection were
performed for many years under contract by private companies"
(p. 27). Seattle has been contracting for residential solid waste removal since 1938 (Hirsch, 1991) and San Francisco since 1932 (President's Commission on Privatization, 1988).

A central issue to remember here is that much of this early
privatization occurred in the environment of limited government
services described above. Market-based approaches to the provision
of goods and services often developed in response to unmet needs,
not to replace existing government services. The "modern movement
toward privatization" (Savas, 1985, p. 17) that began in the late 1970s,
on the other hand, is explicitly designed to substitute privately (or at
least non-publicly) produced goods and services for ones already
being provided in the public sector—"as an alternative to traditional
public bureaucracies" (De Hoog, 1984, p. 4). If one views privatiza-

tion as substitution for existing public services, it is appropriate to speak of privatization as a "relatively recent concept because direct government involvement in the economy is relatively recent too" (Worsnop, 1992, p. 984). Thus, when we describe privatization in this volume, what we are investigating is a "deliberate public policy to improve government" (Savas, 1987, p. 291). Hemming and Mansoor (1988) and Kolderie (1991) provide other ways to separate early privatization initiatives from their more recent relatives.

> The wide range of public sector activities that are now being considered for privatization, the various methods being suggested to achieve this objective, and the enthusiasm with which privatization policy is in some cases being pursued distinguish current privatization efforts from previous ones. (Hemming & Mansoor, 1988, p. 1)

> What is new is the proposal now to expand the practice and to apply it to service areas in which it had not previously been considered. (Kolderie, 1991, p. 254)

*The Seeds of the Modern Movement*

The modern privatization movement as we define it in this volume—that is, the deliberate attempt to shift the allocation and/or the production of services and goods currently in the public domain to the private sector—was foreshadowed by a number of noteworthy events in the quarter century before it took center stage. At the federal level, in 1955, President Eisenhower, through the Bureau of the Budget (the precursor of the Office of Management and Budget [OMB]) became the first president to issue a contracting-out policy (Moore, 1987). According to this policy, federal agencies were issued "directives . . . to procure goods and services from private firms rather than producing them themselves" (Hirsch, 1991, p. 4). Since 1966, when the original policy was replaced by OMB Circular A-76, "the policy has been to utilize outside production whenever doing so saves money, while maintaining necessary service quality" (Hilke, 1992, p. 36). "This new directive requires the Federal agencies to conduct detailed cost comparisons between 'in-house government suppliers' and private vendors. The agency must choose the cheapest alternative" (Moore, 1987, p. 65). Although there is some concern about the way that A-76 may have created an unfair playing field that gives government agencies the advantage (see Moore, 1987), it would, nevertheless, "become familiar as the institutional label for federal-level privatization" (Donahue, 1989, p. 4).

At the state and local level, four events helped give shape to the modern privatization movement. The first was the creation of the "Lakewood Plan" in 1953 (Savas, 1985). Under this plan, Lakewood, California, was incorporated as a city of 60,000 people with only eight employees—employees who acted as contract officers to purchase services from an assortment of suppliers. A second cardinal event was the publication of *The Age of Discontinuity* in 1968 by Peter Drucker. It was here that the term "privatization" originated (Hirsch, 1991; Worsnop, 1992). More significant, it was this volume that laid out the argument "that government should spend more time governing and less time providing" (cited in Fitzgerald, 1988, p. 17).

A snowstorm in New York provided a surprisingly fertile bed for the third seed of the privatization movement at the local level. Fitzgerald (1988) tells the story:

> During John Lindsay's term as mayor of New York, that city's sanitation department took more than a week to clean the streets after a heavy snowstorm in 1969, a delay that produced political problems for the Lindsay administration. One of the mayor's aides, E. S. Savas, an economist, was assigned to investigate why the city department failed to perform efficiently. He began a cost comparison between the city sanitation department and private refuse collectors in the suburbs, finding that it cost the city $49 per ton to remove solid waste compared to only $19 per ton for private firms. As he examined other city services, such as street repair, he found a continuing ratio of about 2.6 to one in city costs over private costs. Later, in a 1971 article for *Harper's*, Savas described how consumers of municipal services are victimized by unresponsive, monopolistic agencies in need of private-sector competition. (p. 7)

Savas's investigation helped fuel the developing debate on rebalancing the public-private service delivery equation.

Finally, there is the catalytic work of Robert Poole, Jr., who helped spread the early seeds of privatization through his Local Government Center and through *Reason* magazine. Again, we turn to Fitzgerald (1988), who has detailed Poole's contributions to the foundations of the modern privatization movement:

> The ideas [of Savas] attracted the attention of a young MIT-trained engineer and systems analyst, Robert W. Poole, Jr., who in 1971 became publisher of *Reason* magazine, a journal of libertarian philosophy, which began to devote articles to the practical applications of privatization. With a recent Harvard graduate, Mark Frazier, Poole in 1976 established the Local Government Center in Santa Barbara, California, to advise municipalities on how to cut budgets. Poole wrote a pamphlet, "How to Cut Local Taxes Without Reducing Essential Services," financed by the National Taxpayer's Union, and later expanded in the book, *Cutting Back City Hall*. Based on a *Reason* article by Poole, CBS's *60 Minutes* aired a program in 1978 on the efficiency and cost-effectiveness of a private fire department serving Scottsdale, Arizona. That segment inspired the formation of at least three new private firefighting companies in other states and brought nationwide attention for the first time to privatization's quiet revolution.
>
> Over in Britain, Poole's book influenced three young men who would rapidly move to the forefront of the privatization debate—Stuart Butler, his brother Eamonn, and Madsen Pirie. They established the Adam Smith Institute in London, dedicated to advancing privatization and free-market ideas. All three had worked for the Heritage Foundation in Washington, D.C., and Stuart Butler became its director of domestic policy studies and a principal proponent of enterprise zones to revitalize inner cities. After Margaret Thatcher's election as Britain's prime minister in 1979, privatization proposals promoted by the Adam Smith Institute became national policy, altering Britain's traditional political debate from whether spending should be cut to the question of whether certain government services and nationalized industries should be moved entirely into the private sector. (pp. 8-9)

## Growth of Privatization:
## The Modern Movement

> The issue of estimating the present extent of privatization is complicated, since the public sector bought a significant amount of goods and services from the private sector long before privatization became an important policy concern. (Hirsch, 1991, p. 4)

> The public sector was much slower to react to changes in its operating environment, and contracting out did not gain notoriety as an approach to service delivery until the late 1970s and early 1980s. (Ascher, 1991, p. 300)

Although it is impossible to date exactly the origin of the modern privatization movement, the period of time from 1975 to 1980 is a reasonable placeholder. Widespread, sustained attention to privatization began to flourish in this period—and has continued throughout the 1980s and 1990s. Chapter 4 investigates the rationale for the advance of privatization. Before we undertake that task, however, it is instructive to review the growth of privatization in the United States at both the state/local and federal levels. Some examples of privatization initiatives unfolding on the world stage are also presented. We begin by reinforcing a central conclusion developed in Chapter 2: When describing privatization in countries outside the United States, we are talking primarily about asset sales and service-shedding. However, because the United States "never had many government enterprises and assets" (Hirsch, 1991, p. 3), privatization here refers overwhelmingly to contracting. The data provided below should be reviewed from this perspective.

### Privatization at the State/Local Level

For a number of reasons, "privatization [in the United States] has been largely a widespread local phenomenon" (Fitzgerald, 1988, p. 9). To begin with, as noted above, nationalization is not a central theme in this economy. Thus, less privatization activity is possible at the federal level. Second, there has been considerable resistance to new privatization initiatives at the federal level (Moore, 1987; Worsnop, 1992). Third, local and state government agencies spend roughly one third more than the federal government (Hilke, 1992):

In short, there is simply more *room* to contemplate shifts toward private suppliers at lower levels of government. Hence it is at the state and, especially the county and municipal levels, that privatization has gained the most attention in recent years. (Donahue, 1989, p. 131)

*Aggregate Patterns.* Beginning with the knowledge that "contracting out in the United States has been employed most widely at the state and local levels" (President's Commission on Privatization, 1988, p. 2), the salient question is: How extensive is the movement? The prevailing sentiment in the literature is that a "comprehensive . . . privatization revolution" (Moore, 1987, p. 62) "has exploded" (Brown, 1991, p. 272) the operational algorithm by which the provision of services is determined. According to many analysts, privatization "has grown tremendously . . . since the early 1970s" (Fixler & Poole, 1987, p. 164) and is steadily "gaining ground" (Seader, 1991, p. 30): "There is moderately strong quantitative evidence that privatization has grown dramatically" (Fixler & Poole, 1991, p. 71) over the past 20 years. These reviewers perceive a privatization "revolution quietly and subtly reshaping America" (Fitzgerald, 1988, p. 18).

Others examining much of the same, as well as some different, data arrive at a more tempered conclusion (Hirsch, 1991; Van Horn, 1991). They maintain that "the surveys done so far are not definitive enough to declare privatization a major trend" (Peters, 1991, p. 59). They argue that the evidence "indicates few dramatic shifts toward greater use of alternative delivery approaches for public services in American local governments" (Renner, 1989, p. 12). As one of the leading proponents of privatization has noted, despite the intellectual acceptance of the concept and "despite the growth rate of contracting and the availability of useful guidelines for all steps involved in contracting, no stampede in this direction is evident" (Savas, 1987, p. 255).

Overall, the judgment about rapid expansion in contracting during the 1970s appears to hold, whereas much more constrained growth marks the period of time from the late 1970s to the mid 1980s—a period of considerable slowdown in the growth of state and local spending (Shannon, 1981). Evidence on the extent of privatization over the past decade is still in the formative stage. Looking at the data in aggregate form, Savas (1987) has concluded that municipal privatization by contracting, in terms of percentage of services contracted to the private sector, grew "from 7 to 26 percent between 1973 and 1982, an average, annual compounded growth rate of 16 percent" (p. 72). In terms of dollars spent, between 1972 and 1982 "the total dollar amount of local government contract awards with private firms about tripled from 22 to 65 billion" (Dudek & Company, 1989, p. 8). "The Council of State Governments notes that in 1982 $81 billion per year of services were provided by the private sector through privatization. That figure was up from $67 billion in 1980 and $27 billion in 1975" (Seader, 1991, p. 31). By 1985, state and local agencies were spending more than $100 billion for private sector delivery of public services (Miller & Tufts, 1991).

As noted above, however, aggregate data suggest that the privatization engine may have cooled considerably after this initial spurt of growth (Miller & Tufts, 1991). Hirsch (1991), for example, maintains that temporary privatization (such as contracting) has "mainly involved relatively small budget items and that the total expenditure has not amounted to much" (p. 33). Donahue (1989) reaches a similar conclusion. In fact, according to his analysis, "the share of state and local budgets that went to goods and services from outside suppliers actually *fell* measurably between 1978 and 1987, from over 40 percent to around 36 percent" (pp. 132-133).

*Patterns by Municipalities and Functions.* Growth in privatization can be assessed in a variety of ways. In addition to those already discussed—amount of services contracted out and dollars spent—the best indicator is a combination measure of the number of government agencies contracting with for-profit and not-for-profit firms and the number of functions privatized. Another approach for which there is insufficient data at the current time to draw conclusions, but will merit attention in the future, is to examine the supply side of contracting—that is, the number of companies that are developed or reshaped to bid for the provision of services historically found in the public sector. For example, in the late 1960s, the first modern-era private fire company was awarded a contract to provide fire protection in Scottsdale, Arizona (Donahue, 1989). "By the mid-1980s there were around half-dozen firms in the industry" (p. 70) such that a "city of up to 150,000-200,000 can issue a request for proposals for fire service and actually have a realistic chance of getting two or three bids from national firms with a track record" (Poole, 1985, p. 47).

Returning to the assessment of the number of municipalities engaged in contracting, the available data are consistent with the story line developed above—rapid expansion from 1972 to 1982 (Clarkson, 1989; Moore, 1987) followed by much more limited growth during the early and mid 1980s (Pack, 1991). Between 1973 and 1982, "the percentage of cities contracting out a wide range of municipal services ranging from refuse collection to data processing, rose dramatically" (Dudek & Company, 1989, p. 51). During this time, local government agencies also "increasingly turn[ed] to the private sector to perform a much wider range of activities" (p. 1):

> Between 1973 and 1982 the number of cities and counties shedding their service-production roles and contracting with private firms escalated rapidly. Street repair went from 63 contracts to 444 a decade later, data-processing contracts from 9 to 337, parks-maintenance contracts from only 5 to 142. Numerous communities have been almost totally privatized, farming-out all service activities except the policy-making and contract-oversight functions of government. (Fitzgerald, 1988, p. 19)

> There is considerable evidence to support impressionistic signs that privatization has grown tremendously in the United States since the early 1970s. Probably the best evidence is provided by a National Center for Policy Analysis (NCPA) comparison of the 1973 survey by the Advisory Commission on Intergovernmental Relations (ACIR) and the 1982 survey by the International City Management Association (ICMA). Although the surveys differed in several respects, including sample size, service definitions, and number of respondents, NCPA's analysis of 17 services covered in both surveys indicates significant growth in at least one privatization method—contracting out with for-profit firms. The NCPA analysis indicated that from 1973 to 1982 the percentage growth ranged from 43 percent for refuse collection to 3,644 percent for data processing (record keeping). (Fixler & Poole, 1991, p. 70)

A comparison of responses to the 1973 ACIR survey and the 1982 ICMA survey indicates a 421 percent increase in the contracting out of legal services. (Fixler & Poole, 1987, p. 167)

A comparison of responses to the 1973 ACIR and the 1982 ICMA surveys indicates that contracting out for recreation facilities increased by a dramatic 1,757 percent. (Fixler & Poole, 1991, p. 73)

Again, comparing responses to the 1973 ACIR and 1982 ICMA surveys, the contracting out of utility billing to for-profit firms increased by some 65 percent over that period. (Fixler & Poole, 1991, p. 74)

A comparison of responses to the 1973 ACIR and 1982 ICMA surveys indicates that the contracting out of hospital management and operation to for-profit firms increased some 53 percent. (Fixler & Poole, 1991, p. 76)

So comprehensive was this activity that in 1987, Moore concluded that "many commercial activities once performed almost exclusively by public employees are now predominantly contracted out" (p. 62). Darr (1991) reached a similar conclusion: "It's clear that more and more functions traditionally performed by public employees are increasingly being turned over to the private sector" (p. 61). Throughout this period, both the number of places and the list of services opening up to the private sector were "continually lengthening" (Dudek & Company, 1989, p. 8). Indeed, by

mid-1987 there were some twenty-eight thousand recorded instances of public services being provided by private firms under contract to local governments. Virtually every function of local government has been delegated to the private sector at some time, in some city. (Donahue, 1989, p. 135)

However, as can be seen in Table 3.3, from the early to the mid 1980s, "the number of places using contracting for various purposes appears to have expanded very little" (Pack, 1991, p. 298). More recent studies on privatization in cities by Roehm et al. (1991) and Worsnop (1992) confirm a pattern of more moderate growth of privatization at the local level throughout the 1980s and early 1990s.

**TABLE 3.3**    Contracting Out by Cities and Counties (percentage of cities or counties with activity)

| Activity | 1982 | 1987 |
|---|---|---|
| Buildings and grounds | 21-23 | 46 |
| Data processing | 23-25 | 38 |
| Administrative services | 49-51 | 40 |
| Fleet and vehicle maintenance | 32 | 23 |
| Solid waste—Collection and disposal | 44 | 77 |
| Streets and roads | 27-28 | 32 |
| Traffic signals and street lighting | 39-41 | 36 |
| Parking lots and garages | 12-14 | 16 |
| Utilities, meter reading | 13-14 | 14 |
| Recreation, parks, etc. | 13-22 | 22 |
| Transportation | 23-46 | 55 |
| Public safety | 5-11 | 7 |
| Housing and shelters | 18-32 | 15 |
| Hospitals and health services | 27-42 | 21 |
| Elderly and handicapped services | 29-37 | 18 |
| Child and day care | 37-78 | 16 |

SOURCE: From Pack, Janet Rothenberg. "The Opportunities and Constraints of Privatization" in Gormley, William T., Jr., ed. *Privatization and Its Alternatives* © 1991. Madison: University of Wisconsin Press. Reprinted by permission of The University of Wisconsin Press.

A historical examination of privatization by function reveals the following: (a) initial forays into privatization focused on "routine support services" (Fixler & Poole, 1991, p. 72), such as janitorial services and plant maintenance; (b) privatization as a policy tool is turned first on those areas "with a lower degree of publicness" (Clarkson, 1989, p. 154); (c) the advantages of adopting privatization are most obvious where "services are well defined and easy to measure" (Hilke, 1992, p. 164); (d) "it is [easier] to extend contracting to intermediate service inputs" (Pack, 1991, p. 298), such as laundry services, than to "final goods and services" (Gormley, 1991a, p. 10), such as education; (e) "privatization has advanced more rapidly in the 'physical and commercial services' [than in] the 'protective and human services'" (p. 9); and, of particular relevance for this volume, (f) there is a recent trend afoot to contract out the delivery of social services (Dudek & Company, 1989), especially to non-profit organizations (Moore, 1987; Savas, 1987). The privatization "debate now focuses sharply on human services, or social services" (Gormley, 1991a, p. 9).

*Privatization at the Federal Level*

> The key on the Federal cash register struck most often has
> been "No Sale." (Smith, 1987, p. 179)

One persistent theme in the literature is that "while most local
governments have embraced privatization to some degree . . . the
Federal government [has] proceeded more cautiously" (Gormley,
1991a, p. 3); "the privatization revolution that is taking place on the
state and local levels is passing the Federal government by" (Moore,
1987, p. 62). Although analysts acknowledge the long tradition of some
federal departments in contracting for services (Hirsch, 1991; Van Horn,
1991), privatization proponents see the lack of growth in privatization at the federal level—particularly when compared to the expansion at the local level—as troublesome (Moore, 1987; Smith, 1987). This
is especially true when the large potential for such activity is considered (Hilke, 1992). In particular, Dudek & Company (1989) decry the
very minimal progress that has been made in transferring to the
private sector the more than one-half million positions "identified as
candidates for contracting out" (p. 2) by the Grace Commission.

Analysts argue that an entrenched bureaucracy, a powerful employee union, self-serving politicians in both the administrative and
legislative branches, and program beneficiaries have coalesced to
impede the advance of privatization efforts at the federal level
(Smith, 1987; Worsnop, 1992). They point out that, more so than at
the local level, federal privatization policies—especially ones relating to contracting out—have been weakened by "increased regulation and mounting restrictions" (Moore, 1987, p. 65).

Nevertheless, although new privatization efforts at the federal
level "fell well short of expectations" (Donahue, 1989, p. 5) during
the 1980s, some advances were made. In 1982, for instance, the
National Consumer Cooperative Bank was cut loose to operate as a
private enterprise (Worsnop, 1992). Conrail—the federally owned
freight carrier—was sold in 1987 for $1.65 billion. At the time,
Elizabeth Dole, then Secretary of Transportation, extolled the sale as
"the largest privatization in U.S. history" (cited in Worsnop, 1992,
p. 989). "Less visible and less symbolically resonant but more important in financial terms was the selling off of five billion dollars in
government loans" (Donahue, 1989, p. 5).

*Privatization on the World Stage*

Although not central to our analysis, it is important at least to acknowledge that the privatization movement is being "fought out on a world canvas" (Bell & Cloke, 1990, p. 24). As Voylsteke (1988), Nankani (1988), Candoy-Sekse (1988), Pirie (1988), and Young (1987) document, privatization is indeed a "worldwide phenomenon" (Young, 1987, p. 190) that is growing in its extent and impact. This "worldwide trend toward privatization has accelerated in the past few years" (President's Commission on Privatization, 1988, p. 4). "It is taking place in seventy countries around the world, a number that expands every year" (Young, 1987, p. 190):

> Privatization has taken its first and biggest hold in Britain. It has, however, spread very rapidly around the world, affect ing the poor countries as well as the rich ones, the backward economies and the advanced ones. It has been employed by both communist and capitalist governments, and by democracies and dictatorships. Its universal applicability may be judged by its ubiquity. It affects countries in the East and the West, in the Northern and Southern Hemispheres, and has touched every continent and even the Pacific Islands. (Pirie, 1988, p. 14)

Because privatization outside the United States is defined primarily in terms of service shedding and asset sales, it is to data on those strategies that we turn to document the extent of privatization. Throughout the world, sales of state-owned enterprises increased from $23 billion in 1985 to $259 billion in 1991 (Worsnop, 1992, p. 991). In Britain, "very much the trail blazer" (Pirie, 1988, p. 3) in this area, "the record of asset sales rose from a modest start of £377 million in 1979/80 to over £5 billion in 1986/87" (Pirie, 1988, p. 3), in the reversal of "a very long post-war process during which the tendency has been for state involvement in both productive and consumptive" (Bell & Cloke, 1990, p. 4) activity. From 1979 to 1987, there was a drop from 11.5% to 7.5% of "gross domestic product accounted for by state-owned enterprises" (Vickers & Yarrow, 1988, p. 1).

In Japan, the state-owned telecommunications system was sold, as were the state tobacco and salt monopolies (Young, 1987).

On the continent of Europe, the French have embarked upon a massive programme of £65 billion of public sector sales. . . . Spain started by selling SEAT, its auto manufacturer. The German government decided to concentrate on industry, transport and banking. Turkey, more adventurously, sold the Keban hydroelectric dam and the Bosporus bridge. Privatization has made itself felt in countries as diverse as Portugal in the south and Sweden in the north. (Pirie, 1988, p. 13)

In Italy, the state holding company "raised 1.59 billion by selling off shares in various enterprises" (Young, 1987, p. 191). Similar stories are being written in Latin American countries, in the former communist bloc nations, and, most dramatically, in the various Asian countries (Young, 1987):

Among newly developing nations there has been extensive use of the privatization techniques. The Pacific Basin countries have moved toward privatizing their telecommunications industries and state airlines, and have targeted lists of state-owned companies for sale. Malaysia has started a major privatization programme, followed closely by Sri Lanka and Singapore. South Korea is proud of its progress with the new approach.

Poorer countries such as Bangladesh and Pakistan have progressed by privatizing individual textile, jute and sugar flour mills. Jamaica has done the same with sugar refining and hotels. South American countries have enabled private investors to buy holdings in state companies, especially oil, banking and electricity. Elsewhere the examples range from an aluminium firm in Costa Rica to banana farms in Belize. Chile has turned its state pensions system into a new type of private insurance company with a public share issue. (Pirie, 1988, pp. 13-14)

## Conclusion

In this chapter, we examined the evolution of privatization as a policy initiative. We devoted considerable space to an analysis of the growth of the public sector. We did so for two reasons. First, much of the foundation of the privatization movement is anchored in a critique of government growth. Second, privatization strategies, to be successful, must acknowledge and address the causes for the rapid expansion of the public sector over the past half-century. In the second half of the chapter, we discussed the development of the modern privatization movement, reviewing early initiatives as well as trends in the growth of privatization across all levels of government. In Chapters 4 and 5, we examine the rationale for the growth of privatization and proceed to unpack the arguments advanced by advocates and opponents of privatization.

## Note

1. Our focus here is on describing the key theories that are often presented to explain the growth of government. Space limitations prevent a full analysis of the explanatory power of the various theories. Useful information in this regard can be gleaned from Berry and Lowery (1987), Borcherding (1977a, 1977b), and Mueller (1989).

# PRESSURES FOR CHANGE | 4

Several major forces, or pressures, are behind the privatization movement: pragmatic, ideological, commercial, and populist. (Savas, 1987, p. 4)

The explanation for privatization's growth has been—and continues to be—constructed from a variety of materials from diverse sources. Not surprisingly, therefore, the privatization edifice takes on different shapes depending on the intellectual and ideological scaffolds employed in the building process. The next two chapters continue the work of uncovering important ideas used in framing privatization as a policy initiative. These ideas are organized into three broad foundations: pressures for privatization in Chapter 4, and the intellectual underpinnings of privatization and the expected benefits of privatization in Chapter 5.

A variety of frames can be used to capture forces pushing privatization onto the policy stage. The strategy employed here is to gather major arguments for privatization into two broad categories —those that illuminate the rising tide of discontent with public provision of goods and services and those that help define an alternative philosophy about the proper role of government in society.

## A Rising Tide of Discontent

People must see that there is a problem first in order to solve something by privatization. (Poole, 1985, p. 47)

I am prepared to conclude that the public sector does not serve most of us very well. (Niskanen, 1994, p. 281)

The political and economic concepts that have traditionally given legitimacy to government actions have come under growing criticism. (President's Commission on Privatization, 1988, p. 229)

### Declining Confidence in the Public Sector

The steady . . . growth of government dating from the 1930s has come under very critical scrutiny in the 1980s. Criticism is based, in part, on widespread citizen concerns over the increasing costs of government. (Hula, 1990b, p. 4)

The privatization movement has drawn support from a wide range of critics of the current scope of government. (President's Commission on Privatization, 1988, p. 239)

#### The Nature of the Discontent

According to many analysts, a "powerful alliance of ideological and commercial interests" (Martin, 1993, p. 2) has turned its guns on the issue of government provision of services. These critics maintain that government in the United States is troubled and is becoming more so. They point to polls revealing widespread dissatisfaction with government, polls that indicate that only 3 in 10 citizens believe that government is operated for the benefit of all citizens (Savas, 1987); one in two citizens believes that the federal government has become so large and so influential that it represents a real and immediate danger to the rights and freedoms of citizens (Urschel, 1995); and only one out of three voters expresses trust in government— down from four out of five in the late 1950s (Savas, 1982). Other chroniclers of this unrest speak of a mounting sense of skepticism— "skepticism about public enterprises" (Fitzgerald, 1988, p. 22) in general and "skepticism as to the ability of government to implement social goals" (Hula, 1990a, p. xiii) in particular. They believe that a "philosophy borne of suspicion for big government may underlie this [privatization] revolution in America" (Fitzgerald, 1988, p. 20).

Still other reviewers discern a "deeper . . . and much more dangerous" (Savas, 1982, p. 1) cynicism toward (Hula, 1990b), distaste for (Donahue, 1989), or "distrust of government and government officials among Americans" (De Hoog, 1984, p. 1). These analysts portray "the electorate's disappointment in activist government" (Hirsch, 1991, p. 1) and the rise and spread of an antigovernment philosophy in the 1970s and 1980s, a time during which the "government plumbed new depths of disfavor" (Donahue, 1989, p. 3). They describe a "fundamental concern that government simply 'doesn't work.' Planning is seen as inadequate, bureaucracy as inefficient and outcomes highly problematic" (Hula, 1990a, p. xiii). They go on to argue that the consent of the governed is being withdrawn to a significant degree (Savas, 1982):

> In short, government has lost the confidence and faith of the people. Cynics and skeptics see government merely as a bumbling bureaucracy interfering with and annoying hard-working, ordinary people while engaging in ever more inconsistent and misguided behavior that is ludicrous when it doesn't hit too close to home. Or else they look on government as an evil to which they have perforce become accustomed, an exploiting force out of control, a horde of self-aggrandizing opportunists—elected officials, civil servants, and unionized public employees alike. (Savas, 1982, p. 1)

In its softest incarnation, this cynicism leads "politicians and citizens alike to argue that government is no longer the solution to everything" (Florestano, 1991, p. 291) and to question the usefulness of much government-initiated activity (Hula, 1990b). At worst, it has nurtured the belief "that government is destined to fail at whatever it does" (Starr, 1991, p. 34).

### Explaining Declining Confidence

*A Cyclical Reaction to Growth.* The important question here is, What accounts for this discontent, skepticism, and antigovernment philosophy that is helping to fuel the privatization movement? Given the cyclical nature of policy development and other value expressions in American society, it should surprise no one to learn that some of this rising tide of dissatisfaction with public sector initiatives can be characterized as a response to the nearly unbroken growth of government over the past three fourths of the twentieth century—a counterreaction to the Progressive philosophy that has dominated the policy agenda for so long (President's Commission on Privatization, 1988).

*Government Intrusiveness.* Another explanation for the public's unhappiness with government is the widespread perception that "government is doing more than it ought to be doing, that is, it is intruding too much into our lives" (Florestano, 1991, p. 291). Critics note that more and more citizens are chafing under the weight and scope of government activity (Meltzer & Scott, 1978; President's Commission on Privatization, 1988). They characterize a government that has gone too far (Hirsch, 1991)—"public ownership that is more extensive than can be justified in terms of the appropriate role of public enterprises in mixed economies" (Hemming & Mansoor, 1988, p. 3). They argue that "government has become involved in the production of goods and services that do not meet the market failure tests" (Pack, 1991, p. 282) and that government agencies have pushed "themselves into areas well beyond governance. They [have] become involved in the business of business" (President's Commission on Privatization, 1988, p. 3). The results are predictable: Government, it is claimed, "acquires a life of its own" (Savas, 1987, p. 3), welfare loss due to collective consumption increases (Oates, 1972), and citizens experience "a growing desire for more individual self-reliance" (Florestano, 1991, p. 295). Expanding numbers of citizens begin to experience "some public sector institutions as controlling rather than enabling, as limiting options rather than expanding them, as wasting rather than making the best use of resources" (Martin, 1993, p. 8).

*Reanalysis of the Rationale for Government Activity.* Contributing to voter dissatisfaction are recent critical analyses of the model of public sector activity developed to support an expanded government presence (President's Commission on Privatization, 1988). The recent spate of socialist and communist government failures in particular has lent support to these reviews (Martin, 1993; Worsnop, 1992). The critique here is of three types. First, when examined as they are put into practice, the assumptions anchoring public sector activity over the past 30 years look much less appealing than they do when viewed in the abstract (i.e., conceptually). Indeed, "many of the assumptions and predictions on which the earlier growth of government was based have proved either to be false or at least to be subject to much greater doubt" (President's Commission on Privatization, 1988, pp. 249-250). Thus, "part of the account of the retreat of state power since 1979 relies on the way in which its limitations had by then become evident" (Pirie, 1988, p. 16). Foundational propositions, such as the nonpolitical nature of public sector activities, have come under attack as it has been determined that "decisions affecting the economy [are often] made on political grounds instead of economic grounds" (Savas, 1987, p. 8). On the other hand, much of the critique of the market economy upon which public sector growth has been justified, especially "market failure as a sufficient rationale for public intervention" (Pack, 1991, p. 282), has been called into question.

Second, as explicated more fully below, "structural weaknesses inherent in the nature of public-sector supply itself . . . which undermine the whole basis on which it is established" (Pirie, 1988, p. 20) have become more visible—visible to the point that, as Martin (1993) notes, some advocates claim that "state ownership and management are intrinsically flawed" (p. 139). Concomitantly, "both the efficiency and effectiveness of public sector activities [have begun] to be questioned seriously" (Hemming & Mansoor, 1988, p. 1).

Third, it is suggested that the reforms that created the large public sector "are themselves sorely in need of reform, as mistakes, excess, waste, and scandals appear[ed] and the inevitable institutional arteriosclerosis set in" (Savas, 1982, p. 2). Reform is increasingly seen in terms of alternatives to, rather than the repair of, the existing public sector.

*Poor Performance of the Public Sector.* At the core of the discontent is the developing belief that government is not working well—that it is the poor performance of the public sector itself that is leading both to the abandonment of the assumptions used to forge a strong public sector and to calls for a rebalancing of the public-private equation (Pirie, 1988; Savas, 1982). The sentiment that government is becoming increasingly ineffective and inefficient is expressed along a continuum, from those who read the evidence as a mandate for a reduced public sector to those "advocates [who] want us to think about government as irredeemably incompetent [and prefer] to empty out the portfolio of public responsibilities" altogether (Starr, 1991, p. 35).

Certainly, part of the belief "that too many of our Government agencies are failing our people" (President's Commission on Privatization, 1988, p. 3) can be traced to an overly optimistic picture— or uncritical acceptance—of the benefits of government intervention. Government employees are not, for example, simply the self-effacing, other-oriented agents that the literature portrays (Tullock, 1994a). Concomitantly, social problems are much more intractable than many supporters of an interventionist government believed was the case (Goldring & Sullivan, 1995)—"legitimate societal aspirations once thought attainable only by big government have proven [elusive]" (Savas, 1987, p. 278).

The perceived failure of the public sector is, however, more broadly anchored. Often grounded in stories of gross government incompetence or scandal, a body of evidence is mounting that "public enterprises are often inefficient and incur losses" (Hemming & Mansoor, 1988, p. 1)—that it costs more to accomplish tasks in the government than in the private sector. Or, stated alternatively, government is consuming more of the nation's resources than it should: "The government provision and production of many goods and services, including the regulation of market activities, generates substantial deadweight losses" (De Alessi, 1987, p. 24). Although "widespread concern over the increasing costs of government" (Hula, 1990b, p. 4) is an important variable in the algorithm of discontent—especially perceived "waste and inefficiency" (Poole, 1985, p. 46)—an even more significant factor is the expanding disillusionment about "the overall effectiveness of government action" (Hula, 1990b, p. 4), particularly the perceived inability of government to meet its goals. Perhaps nowhere is this perception more vivid than in the arena of the large-scale egalitarian programs of the 1960s and 1970s (Hula, 1990b). A number of critics of activist government argue that the conditions that led to the development of these policies have not been ameliorated, and they will "not disappear as a result of having responsibility for them transferred from the private to the public sector" (Savas, 1987, p. 290). In fact, they maintain that such transfers "often aggravate the situation and create even more problems" (p. 290). They go so far as to suggest that many of our social problems are in reality cratogenic, that is, created by the state. One powerful example of this phenomenon, they say, is the public housing sector. Nearly $8 billion per year is spent on public housing assistance. According to Fitzgerald (1988), however, "public housing tenants receive only 34 cents from every tax dollar spent, with the sponge of government absorbing the rest" (p. 38). The result is a system of housing widely acknowledged as deplorable as well as there being "little evidence that the programs [have] succeeded at anything other than making poor people more dependent on government" (p. 30). Critics offer similar stories about the failure of other domains of public sector activity (e.g., prisons and education) to achieve important social goals.

*Disgruntlement With Bureaucracy.* As will be discussed more fully in Chapter 5, the perceived failure of the public sector is often traced to the door of government bureaucracy: "Although almost all areas and levels of government have been the object of criticism, the government bureaucracies have probably received the loudest, largest, and most vociferous criticism" (De Hoog, 1984, p. 1). The basic reasoning of some analysts is that public bureaucracies are characterized by "irritating methods and unsatisfactory performance" (Niskanen, 1971, p. 18); are "prone to failure" (Gormley, 1991a, p. 6; see especially Downs, 1967; Peirce, 1981); and "sap efficiency" (Donahue, 1989, p. 123). De Hoog (1984) observes that disapproval with bureaucracy takes two basic forms. First, as indicated above, many citizens—and the business sector—express "a fear of the growing government bureaucracy interfering in and controlling many aspects of life" (p. 2). Second, there is an increasing "dissatisfaction with the public bureaucracies' implementation of programs . . . and provision of services" (p. 2). Supporting this discontent is the recasting of government officials in the public choice literature from "textbook figures pursuing an idealized public interest" (Fixler & Poole, 1987, p. 177) to "bureaucrats [who] are more interested in their own well-being than in the public interest" (Tullock, 1994a, p. 97) and who "tend to adopt policies that will ease their work load and make their jobs more pleasant" (Hanke, 1985, p. 6). The outcome of this, not surprisingly, is that "privatization's appeal owes much to the dream of stripping away the red tape that festoons bureaucratic undertakings" (Donahue, 1989, p. 128). As Niskanen (1994) argues, "efficiency in government cannot be much improved without changing the basic institutions and processes that affect the demand for and supply of government-financed services" (p. 275).

*Unhappiness With the Wealth Transfer Aspects of Government.* The discontent with and expanded skepticism about public sector activity are reinforced by a growing suspicion that government intervention is becoming less an instrument to provide services to the general citizenry and more and more a vehicle to transfer income and wealth to individuals and groups (Donahue, 1989). Such transfers are of three types: (a) income and benefit premiums ("rents" in the economics lexicon) available to government employees—that is, additional income and benefits enjoyed by civil servants compared to that received by employees in comparable jobs in the private sector; (b) affirmative action employment policies that shift wealth in the direction of targeted groups of citizens; and (c) particular programs that are created primarily to redistribute income.

Discontent is also heightened by the perceived inability of the public sector to heal itself, or, more precisely, by the failure of a plethora of off-budget and modern business strategies to improve the performance of the public sector (Pirie, 1985). As Savas (1987) notes:

> The history of modern government is replete with efforts to improve government by centralizing, decentralizing, reorganizing, introducing performance budgeting, PPBS (planning-programming-budgeting systems), ZBB (zero-based budgeting), MBO (management by objectives), management training, sensitivity training, organization development, worker incentives, shared savings, labor-management committees, productivity councils, computerization, management science, operations research, and numerous other techniques. (p. 5)

The results have been modest at best, leading analysts of the process to conclude

> that trying to bring private sector disciplines into the public sector is tantamount to attempting to graft an alien growth. It is much easier to move the operation into the private sector

> where it will be exposed to those disciplines anyway. (Pirie, 1985, p. 56)

Thus,

> privatization has become an attractive idea these days be-
> cause the reform that can readily be seen as an alternative to
> privatization—transforming government itself—appears to
> be much more difficult than the process of contracting out to
> a private concern. (Frug, 1991, p. 307)

This widespread dissatisfaction with government and public sector activity has led some to question "whether public production . . . is so inherently inefficient that it results in even greater resource misallocation than do the market failures it aims to correct; whether regulation is even more costly to society than the initial resource misallocations" (Pack, 1991, p. 282). In tangible terms, it has helped foster a taxpayer revolt and has given birth to an array of citizen initiatives designed to seize control from existing government structures. At the core of these reactions is the "feeling that there must be a better way of doing all those things that governments do not do too well" (Savas, 1985, p. 17): "If government is failing in its efforts to provide essential services, should we not reconsider the role we have given government in these areas?" (Carroll, Conant, & Easton, 1987, p. x). For some, especially given the lack of success accruing from strategies to reform or buttress the public sector, "a more fundamental strategic approach is needed" (Savas, 1987, p. 5). For many in this group, one particular avenue of change—privatization—looks especially promising: "If we desire to improve efficiency and eliminate public sector waste, we must change property rights arrangements by adopting privatization policies" (Hanke, 1985, p. 8).

### Fiscal Stress

> Perhaps the most critical factor that pushed cities and states
> to privatize was prolonged and intense budgetary pressures.
> The financial condition of most state and local governments
> during the late 1970s and early 1980s was singularly bleak.
> (Moore, 1987, p. 69)

Unquestionably, one of the key factors contributing to the popularity of privatization has been "the growing cost-revenue squeeze on government" (Fixler & Poole, 1987, pp. 176-177): "In the late 1970s and throughout the 1980s . . . officials became squeezed between escalating demands of constituents—coupled with rising claims by public employees' unions—and the reality of fixed or declining budgets" (Donahue, 1989, p. 131). Indeed, the period when privatization was breaking over the political landscape corresponds exactly to the era when states and cities were "experienc[ing] all at once almost every conceivable fiscal nightmare" (Moore, 1987, p. 70) and a severe "deterioration in fiscal conditions" (Dudek & Company, 1989, p. 9), including their own vulnerability to bankruptcy (Ross, 1988). Such problems included political, judicial, and constitutional restrictions on their ability to raise funds; taxpayer revolts; restrictions in federal and state aid; double-digit inflation; a sobering economic recession; heightened demands for public services; increased interest in using the public sector to support political goals; and rising demands by public employees (Darr, 1991; Donahue, 1989; Dudek & Company, 1989; Moore, 1987; Peters, 1991; Renner, 1989). With this new era of fiscal strain, "the more predictable days of local government" (Kemp, 1991, p. 1) disappeared, and pragmatism and expediency (De Alessi, 1987; Donahue, 1989) moved to center stage as government officials attempted "to extricate themselves from the bind of limited resources and the constant or increasing demand for services" (Kolderie & Hauer, 1991, p. 87).

*Cost Dimension*

One side of the equation of fiscal pressure highlights the demand for services and the costs of those activities. Indeed, Van Horn (1991) has shown that "the inability to meet rising demands for services, rather than the fear of budget cutbacks or the desire for efficiency, has goaded several large and rapidly growing departments into using private contractors" (p. 268). At the outset, it is important to note that the reasons for the rapid expansion of the public sector outlined in Chapter 3 remain. The conditions pressing for government services have not been diminished. If anything, a "confluence of demographic, legal, and political trends" (Donahue, 1989, p. 151) has exacerbated demands for public services. A number of dynamics are at work here. Public expectations of government services are heightened during periods of economic hardship, such as the recessions of the 1970s and 1980s (Kemp, 1991). It is also during such periods that union resistance to trimming the government workforce tends to be most strident. At the same time, states and municipalities are being hit by expanding requirements for services from Congress and from the executive branch of the federal government—especially regarding environmental issues (Seader, 1991)—as well as from federal and state courts (e.g., demands to eliminate prison overcrowding) even as federal revenues are declining. Finally, "growing financial responsibilities" (Hirsch, 1991, p. 15) are being fed by a "combination of client advocates, the media, and the political process [that] work[s] powerfully to turn needs into rights, rights into entitlements, entitlements into programs, and programs into budgets" (Kolderie, 1991, p. 259).

*Revenue Dimension*

"Much of the current impetus to the cutback of government programmes is tied to revenue issues" (Hula, 1990b, p. 4). This revenue side of the cost-revenue squeeze—the lack of funds or shrinking budget side—is composed of two issues: decreased tax revenues and "less generous and less reliable federal aid than in the past" (Worsnop, 1992, p. 979). As a number of scholars have concluded, "reduced transfers of funds from the federal government . . . and growing hostility to increased taxes" (Hanke, 1985, p. 3) have "worked powerfully to constrain the resources that come into the economy and the amount available for public service provision" (Kolderie, 1991, p. 259).

Tax pressures associated with the taxpayers' revolt and the tax limitation measures of the 1970s and 1980s represent one aspect of the revenue constraint (Ascher, 1991; Roehm et al., 1991). This "popular resistance to higher taxes" (Worsnop, 1992, p. 990) has acted both as a mechanism to reduce the public coffers and as "an antidote to demands for government services" (Savas, 1982, p. 16). Although there are differences of opinion as to the vitality of taxpayer resistance, many reviewers believe that "there is considerable evidence that taxpayers are dissatisfied with either the current level of taxation or with the level of public services provided by all levels of government in relation to taxes" (Bennett & Johnson, 1980, p. 363). Indeed, by 1990, "about half the states [had] enacted revenue limitation and/or expenditure limitation laws such as Propositions 13 and 4 in California and Proposition 1½ in Massachusetts" (Hirsch, 1991, p. 15).

At the same time that municipalities have been experiencing the constraints of limited tax revenues, they have also been subject to a curtailment of federal aid in the form of intergovernmental grants (Donahue, 1989; Fitzgerald, 1988; Renner, 1989):

> On the federal level, funding for domestic programs was cut significantly and fiscal resources previously available to state and local government for funding services were reduced. Federal action not only included a reduction in funding of domestic services that were previously considered to be federal responsibilities but also reduced grants to state and local governments. Federal grants as a percent of public sector funds declined from 10.3 percent in 1979 to 7.1 percent in 1987. (Hirsch, 1991, p. 15)

It is also hypothesized that the ongoing struggle to address the budget deficit "will continue cutbacks in numerous federal assistance programs, including general revenue sharing" (Scader, 1991, p. 32) and will thereby "continue to exacerbate the financial plight of our local governments" (Kemp, 1991, p. 8).

*Infrastructure Crisis*

A particularly troublesome dimension of the fiscal squeeze being experienced by state and local governments—and one that intersects with both cost and revenue strands—is the "infrastructure crisis" (Gomez-Ibanez et al., 1990, p. 172), or "the mounting problem of 'crumbling' infrastructure" (Worsnop, 1992, p. 992). According to most observers, "Local governments are facing a common dilemma —an enormous need for infrastructure facilities without the financial wherewithal to fund their construction" (Goldman & Mokuvos, 1991, p. 25). The demand for these capital projects, both for repair of existing structures and the production of new ones, is continuing to mount:

> Our infrastructure-repair needs already far exceed our willingness or ability to pay. Bridges and highways are deteriorating faster than we can replace or rehabilitate them—the

cost of just maintaining highway conditions to the year 2000 will be $324 billion, a figure the U.S. Department of Transportation concedes does not include bridge maintenance or necessary new highway construction. We have legislated ourselves another layer of unfunded liability under the Clean Water Act, which the Environmental Protection Agency estimates will require $120 billion just to provide immediate sewage treatment mandated by the law. Altogether, across the entire spectrum of infrastructure needs, the Joint Economic Committee of Congress has calculated the shortage of funds at $1.1 trillion by the year 2000. (Fitzgerald, 1988, p. 13)

While the demands for more and better infrastructure, as well as for capital to fuel development of that infrastructure (Seader, 1991), are increasing, the ability (or willingness) of municipalities to pay for new facilities is failing to keep pace:

Yet the CBO estimates spending on infrastructure to be only $39 billion annually, or $624 billion by the end of the century, creating an infrastructure "gap" of between $236 billion and $486 billion. (Fitzgerald, 1988, p. 13)

Although the financial health of most U.S. municipalities has improved markedly during the 1980s, cities almost certainly will not be capable of raising the tens of billions of dollars of capital that will be needed for the rehabilitation of such facilities as transit systems, wastewater treatment plants, hospitals, roads, bridges, and airports. (Dudek & Company, 1989, p. 8)

As a result, because they "limit or avoid large capital expenditures" (Roehm et al., 1991, p. 280), "creative financing techniques available through privatization are . . . becom[ing] an increasingly attractive option" (Dudek & Company, 1989, p. 8) for the "environmental, social and economic development needs [of] municipalities without the monetary means to finance infrastructure facilities" (Goldman & Mokuvos, 1991, p. 28). Furthermore, privatization advocates claim that

because the private sector has unique advantages available to it that are not available to local governments, public officials have the opportunity to capitalize on situations that could result in savings for the community. The possible savings result from construction cost and time efficiencies, operational advantages, and utilization of tax benefits. (Goldman & Mokuvos, 1991, p. 25)

Some reviewers contend that the noneconomic benefits that will accrue from private sector involvement in infrastructure development include (a) "risk sharing, especially for environmental facilities where the private sector takes responsibility for providing, owning, and operating sewage treatment plants or other environmental control facilities" (Seader, 1991, p. 32); (b) reduction in liability; and (c) the ability to secure expertise or "specialized skills and resources that may be unavailable within the government" (Dudek & Company, 1989, p. 1).

### The Privatization Safety Valve

All this fiscal stress has resulted in governments experiencing difficulty in providing the array of goods, services, and facilities that citizens need (Seader, 1991). Along with the rising tide of discontent with public sector activities, fiscal pressures have provided a wake-up call to public agencies, many of whom "are having to reconsider once again how they pursue their fundamental purposes" (Fitzgerald et al., 1990, p. 70), including "searching for new ways of delivering services" (Peters, 1991, p. 53). As various analysts have noted, "when governments face severe fiscal stress, that is, when the cost of government activities is rising but the public's resistance to higher taxes is also rising, public officials seek any promising solution to their quandary" (Savas, 1987, p. 4)—"any alternative delivery mechanism that might allow government to achieve more with less money" (Van Horn, 1991, p. 263). Many reformers are looking for "new funding methods for traditional service delivery" (Seader, 1991, p. 32), turning to the market—or "private provision of public goods and services" (Wilson, 1990, p. 59)—for help. Specifically, "all across the country revenue-pinched governments are turning to private firms as a way of saving money without impairing the delivery of services" (Worsnop, 1992, p. 977). As Dudek & Company (1989) remind us, this connection has not been drawn by chance: "It is no accident that the rapid adoption of contracting out as an acceptable government management technique coincided with a period of unparalleled financial strain" (p. 9). For many reformers, the appeal to the market offers real promise of solving the fiscal crises. On the political side of the equation, they argue that the "shift of responsibility for service provision from public servants to private markets provides a political buffer against public discontent in an era of fiscal restraint and economic restructuring and an administrative buffer against service accountability" (Ismael, 1988, p. 3) while providing some hope that confidence in government can be restored. On the economic front is the lure of the "significant cost savings potential of privatization" (Fixler & Poole, 1987, p. 165).

## A New Wind Blowing

This is the nub of the ideological case for privatization. The public sector is inherently incapable of doing anything well and should be dismantled. Economic and social policy should not be the concern of politics at all, but left to the market. (Martin, 1993, p. 51)

Privatization is an effort to channel political debate. The intent is not just to improve the efficiency of particular services, but to change aspirations in our society to direct them into the market and out of the arena of politics and the sphere of common responsibility. (Starr, 1991, p. 35)

Analysts on both sides of the privatization debate acknowledge that "privatization is more a *political* than an *economic* act" (Savas, 1987, p. 233): "It is not possible to discuss privatization as if it consisted of techniques and not of ideas. . . . Privatization comes to us in a political bundle, not logically, but ideologically connected" (Starr, 1991, p. 26). A review of the literature in this area shows that privatization represents a particular "public philosophy" (Van Horn, 1991, p. 262), and that advocates of privatization fall into a distinctive ideological camp. As we described in Chapter 1, debates on the usefulness of this public policy instrument often amount to little more than the deployment of amassed "ideological weaponry" (Martin, 1993, p. 45).

## A Shift to the Right

> Dominant ideologies can change over time. In recent years, for example, the apparent resurgence of conservatism, libertarianism (or classical liberalism), and free-market ideas (especially among economists) encourages a more serious consideration of turning over public services to the marketplace. (Fixler, 1991, p. 44)

Privatization draws strength from "a general political movement toward the right" (Brazer, 1981, p. 21) and the fact that "Americans have turned to conservatives for the answers to the most important problems facing the U.S." (Pines, 1985, p. v). The fusion of a political agenda increasingly dominated by "conservative politics" (Martin, 1993, p. 46) and an "economic theology . . . undergoing a return to fundamentalism" (Thayer, 1987, p. 165) has given birth to the doctrine of neoliberalism (Seldon, 1987) and to "the ideological and profit-oriented agenda of the New Right" (Martin, 1993, p. 182)—"the conservative view of government as an economic blackhole" (Starr, 1987, p 126). In the process, "an ideology which has long lurked in the darkest shadows of right-wing thinking [has been] transfer[red] into an apparatus at the very centre of the policy process" (Bell & Cloke, 1990, p. 4).

Undergirding privatization, then, are a particular set of values and political goals and a specific "concept of the relationship between the individual and the state" (Martin, 1993, p. 48). Economic growth and individual choice are the movement's predominant goals, and the market, which is seen as "consistently and wholly benign" (Martin, 1993, p. 47), is touted as the best vehicle to secure those objectives. Not surprisingly, the "language of 'choice' and 'empowerment' " (Martin, 1993, p. 188) is woven throughout the privatization literature: "People should have more choice in public services. They should be empowered to define and address common needs" (Savas, 1987, p. 4). Alternative approaches to government intervention and bureaucratic structures, it is argued, must "buttress individual liberties" (De Alessi, 1987, p. 24)—they must minimize interference with individual freedom and the market (Martin, 1993).

Earlier, it was explained that, when viewed through a pragmatic lens, privatization is about the more efficient delivery of higher quality goods and services. However, "as an ideological principle privatization equals smaller government, lower taxes, and less government intervention in public affairs" (Van Horn, 1991, p. 261). Fueled by citizen discontent with activist government and fiscal stress, newly formed conservative winds are pushing society away from the agenda of the Progressive era and toward a "reconstructing [of] the liberal democratic state" (Starr, 1991, p. 25). The two pillars of this reconstruction are a critique of interventionist government and a renewed faith in the power of markets.

## A New Infatuation With Markets

> Two political legacies of the 1980s will color and constrain the economic policies of the 1990s. [One] is the virtually worldwide cooling toward collectivism. [Another] is a renewed cultural enthusiasm for private enterprise. (Donahue, 1989, p. 3)

### Backlash Against Government

The analysis so far has already captured much of the emerging populist view against large government. On one hand, there has been a weakening of the Progressive vision and a lessening of the influence of Progressive philosophy—a widespread "reaction against the theories and results of Progressive thought" (President's Commission on Privatization, 1988, p. 230), focusing particularly upon the appropriateness of public provision of goods and services that are highly redistributive in nature. Thus, privatization is seen "as a means to get rid of 'dependency culture' " (Martin, 1993, p. 48). Critics argue that "government is too big, too powerful, too intrusive in people's lives and therefore is a danger to democracy" (Savas, 1987, p. 5). This critique of large government is grounded in an analysis of interest group government and "the excess of current interest group politics" (President's Commission on Privatization, 1988, p. 233)—of "distant and unresponsive organs of government" (Savas, 1987, p. 7); "meddling by ministers and civil servants" (Bell & Cloke, 1990, p. 14); groups that are "able to use the political system to secure and maintain benefits at the general expense" (Pirie, 1988, p. 58); and programs that "have too often operated mainly to enlarge the income, status, and power of the industry of bureaucratic and professional service producers, whether governmental or private" (Kolderie, 1991, p. 259). The backlash against government is also driven by the "deficit-induced imperative to limit government spending" (Donahue, 1989, p. 3), which is the fiscal stress rationale outlined above.

Finally, consistent with an increasingly popular libertarian philosophy, there is an ongoing reassessment of the appropriate size of government in general and particular units of government specifically (Tullock, 1988); an emerging "belief that small is beautiful when applied to domestic government" (Fitzgerald, 1988, p. 21); and a rekindling of belief in the appropriateness of self-help and local initiative, especially of "traditional local institutions" (Savas, 1987, p. 10). These winds are blowing us in the direction of decentralization, a "rebuilding America from the bottom up—and the trend away from reliance on political institutions in favor of individual self-help initiatives" (Fitzgerald, 1988, p. 16). New attention is being devoted to "the potential of 'mediating structures' " (Savas, 1987, p. 239)— and the deleterious effects of large government on these structures— that are situated between "the individual and the mechanism of government" (Fitzgerald, 1988, p. 26), such as families, churches, neighborhood groups, and voluntary associations. According to proponents of privatization, based on the belief that "creative local initiatives, informal person-to-person efforts, local role models, and intracommunity pressures are more likely to be effective than bureaucrats" (Savas, 1987, p. 239), "we are witnessing the revival of self-help strategies and voluntarism as expressions of independence from government" (Fitzgerald, 1988, p. 26).

*The Expansion of Pro-Market Forces*

Critique of large government represents the negative case for the dismantling of the liberal democratic state. It is balanced on the positive side by the growing belief that "free market economics provide the path to prosperous equilibrium" (Thayer, 1987, p. 168)— by "the political pendulum swing toward market-oriented solutions" (Seader, 1991, p. 32). Supported by the intellectual pillars of market theory and theories of the firm and by the public choice literature, there is a "new spirit of enterprise in the air" (Hardin, 1989, p. 16)—a renewed interest in "private market values" (Bailey, 1987, p. 141) and in the "virtues of private property" (Hirsch, 1991, p. 2) and a "pro-market trend" (President's Commission on Privatization, 1988, p. 237) in the larger society.

Although analysts are quick to point out the fallacy of this emerging belief in the infallibility of private business (Baber, 1987) and to remind us that "idealization of the market's invisible hand has served to conceal the grubbier ones directing it" (Martin, 1993, p. 6), there is little doubt that the privatization movement is anchored firmly on "belief in the superiority of free market forms of social organization over the forms of social organization of the Keynesian welfare state society" (Ian Taylor, cited in Martin, 1993, p. 48). This expanding reliance on the market moves individuals in the direction of "exercis[ing] choice as consumers rather than as citizens" (Starr, 1991, p. 27). It leads organizations to emulate current private sector business practices, especially the practice of outsourcing. Thus, according to Ascher (1991), privatization via

> contracting out cannot be viewed as a unique political development but must be seen as part of a larger economic trend. Contracting out in the public sector and outsourcing in the private are much like fraternal twins—born of the same parents but with different names and appearances. (p. 301)

The expansion of pro-market sentiment is powered to some extent by the picture painted by some of "a bloated, parasitic public sector blocking the bustle and growth of a more free flowing private economy" (Starr, 1987, p. 124). Two beliefs are central to this line of reasoning: (a) that "the structural organization of the public sector itself" (Pirie, 1988, p. 34) is flawed and (b) that political decisions "are inherently less trustworthy than free-market decisions" (Savas, 1987, p. 5). Starting from here, we find that many analysts are adopting an increasingly skeptical stance on the usefulness of government intervention (Tullock, 1988, 1994a, 1994b). Their revisiting the case for public action (Fixler, 1991) "has caused mainstream economists in recent years to narrow significantly the circumstances thought to require government intervention to correct market failings" (President's Commission on Privatization, 1988, p. 237). Accompanying this reconsideration of the case for public action has been a reanalysis of the supposed problems of markets and, according to privatization advocates, a recognition that because "market forces can find ways round or through vested interests" (Seldon, 1987, p. 133), "the regulation which the market imposes in economic activity is superior to any regulation which rulers can devise and operate by law" (Pirie, 1988, p. 10)—a feeling that because "the level of efficiency of government action is apt to be low, and the possibility of damage through erratic, ill-informed decisions is great, government action should be resorted to only when the social cost emanating from the market is quite great" (Tullock, 1988, p. 103).

## The Quest for New Business

The reasons [for privatization] lie not only in the public sector's own failings, but also in the pursuit of new markets by large corporations. (Martin, 1993, p. ii)

While the debate about privatizing production . . . has its ideological side, most of it is intensely practical. It is very much a clash between competing producers, both of which want the government's business. (Kolderie, 1991, p. 254)

So far, we have examined what might best be thought of as the economic, political, and ideological foundations of privatization. There is still one cornerstone to be considered, however—one that Savas (1987) refers to as "commercial pressure" (p. 9) to dismantle government initiatives in a wide array of areas. According to this line of analysis, as the United States moves from the industrial to the postindustrial era, corporate growth through traditional paths becomes less and less viable. Expansion in the information age must, perforce, be concentrated in the service area, exactly the major domain of government operations. Analysts perceive that this public service sector "offers lucrative new markets" (Darr, 1991, p. 66) for American corporations. They also "see substantial business opportunities in large capital projects" (Savas, 1987, p. 9) needed to address the infrastructure crisis chronicled above.

Education is an especially appealing target for profit-oriented firms for a number of reasons (Murphy, 1993a). To begin with, it is a huge market, with spending on K-12 education alone approaching $250 billion annually. Of that amount, $8.3 billion is spent on student transportation, $8 billion on the school food program, $9 billion on the cleaning and maintenance of school plant, and $10.7 billion on the construction and modernization of school facilities (Beales &

O'Leary, 1993). In addition, there has been relatively little penetration of the education market by the private sector to date. Finally, for many parts of the educational enterprise, start-up costs are far from prohibitive.

On the international level—and especially in developing nations, "where the industrial sector and, occasionally, key elements of the commercial sector, are heavily dominated by public enterprises" (Hemming & Mansoor, 1988, p. 1)—privatization has the potential to open massive new markets for transnational corporations. Leading critics of this process characterize the opening of these foreign markets to large corporations as a type of new colonialism (Hardin, 1989; Martin, 1993), a situation in which "power [is] switched from a remote autocratic state to even more remote institutions that call the shots about economic and social policy just as autocratically" (Martin, 1993, p. 101). Whether the critics are right or not, there is no gainsaying the fact that privatization throughout the world economy opens markets valued at hundreds of billions of dollars to private corporations.

## Conclusion

This chapter began an analysis of the increasing popularity of privatization as a policy instrument. In the first half of the chapter, we examined forces that help explain significant citizen discontent with public sector initiatives. We chronicled the nature of that declining confidence and provided explanations for its spread. We also described the fiscal squeeze in which many government agencies find themselves, reviewing how both cost and revenue issues contribute to this fiscal strain. The second half of the chapter was devoted to an analysis of emerging, or reemerging, political and economic trends that support the philosophy of privatization. In particular, we described a shift to the right in the political arena and a reemphasis on the more fundamental pillars of capitalism, especially the growing infatuation with markets.

The next chapter continues to analyze the rationale of the privatization movement and focuses on two topics—the intellectual scaffolding for privatization and the outcomes, especially the gains, that are expected to flow from privatization initiatives. Chapter 6 discusses the issue of forces promoting privatization in education.

# INTELLECTUAL UNDERPINNINGS AND EXPECTED BENEFITS | 5

The single most important message that public choice has to teach [is that] the rules of the games *do* affect the outcomes of the game. Institutions matter. (Mueller, 1989, p. 346)

This chapter continues the attempt to understand privatization as a strategy for the delivery of services traditionally housed in the government sector, especially education. We begin by examining the theoretical grounding on which privatization is built. We group that discussion into two categories, economic considerations and political activity. We then turn our attention to more practical aspects of privatization—the benefits and costs that are expected to accrue from privatization initiatives. Specifically, we review four categories that can be employed to investigate market-oriented approaches to school reform: efficiency, quality, effects on employees, and values.

## Theoretical Foundations

The theoretical argument for privatization rests on a competitive model to demonstrate the efficiency of private production, and a public choice government failure model wherein the public sector does too much and does it inefficiently. (Pack, 1991, p. 287)

The theoretical grounding of privatization comes from either public-choice theorists, students of monopolistic behavior in economics, or political scientists with a prescriptive view of interest-group analysis. (Bailey, 1991, p. 233)

At the outset of this project, a conscious effort was made to integrate the intellectual foundations of privatization throughout the various sections of the book. Thus, we have already covered a good deal of this territory in earlier chapters. In the forthcoming analysis of the benefits and costs of privatization, we also will have a good deal to say about the theoretical propositions to which privatization policies are tethered. At the risk of some redundancy, it is important to put these foundational issues on center stage, at least briefly, as we shall do in this chapter.

Nearly the entire case for privatization—as well as most of the case against government provision of services—can be found in the body of scholarship known as the public choice literature, a collection of intellectual traditions that developed into a distinctive field around 1950 (Mueller, 1989). According to Buchanan (1989), "public choice is a *perspective* on politics that emerges from an extension and application of the tools and methods of the economist to collective or nonmarket decision making" (p. 13); it is a development in which "basic assumptions underlying economic analysis are transferred to the political realm" (Tullock, 1994a, p. 88). Or, stated more dramatically, "public choice is, essentially, an invasion of political science by the economists" (Tullock, 1988, p. 1). More concretely, public choice is concerned with "the politics of bureaucracy" (Tullock, 1965, p. 10) and "the political economy of representative government" (Niskanen, 1971, p. 12). Of central importance is the fact that "a particular approach to economics" (Buchanan, 1989, p. 13) anchors public choice theory—"an analysis of the behavior of individuals . . . in collective activity . . . in terms of an economic calculus" (Buchanan & Tullock, 1962, p. 21). Specifically, "the basic behavioral postulate of public choice . . . is that man is an egoistic, rational, utility maximizer" (Mueller, 1989, p. 2). For purposes of organization only, we group the arguments of public choice analysts into two clusters: an economic dimension (the advantages of competitive markets and profit incentives) and a political dimension (the dynamics of nonmarket decision making).

## Economic Dimension

> The economic case for privatization is made by reference to public ownership that is more extensive than can be justified in terms of the appropriate role of public enterprises in mixed economies, the poor economic performance of public enterprises compared with private enterprises, and the inherent characteristics of public ownership that give rise to inefficiency. (Hemming & Mansoor, 1988, p. 3)

The economic dimension of public choice theory is anchored by distinct but related lines of scholarship on such issues as private property theory and market theory—scholarship that skeptics of public choice claim presents "an idealized economic foundation" (De Hoog, 1984, p. 24) that makes suspect many claims about the benefits of privatization (Hardin, 1989; Martin, 1993; Starr, 1991; Thayer, 1987; Van Horn, 1991).

### Property Rights Theory

Analysts who come to privatization via property rights theory maintain "that the essential difference between private and public service delivery is the property rights arrangements that underlie each approach" (Fixler, 1991, p. 47). The central proposition is that "changes in property rights will materially affect the incentive structures" (Vickers & Yarrow, 1988, p. 3)—"that private property ownership entails incentives that give private providers an almost inherent superiority over public providers" (Fixler, 1991, p. 47). The embedded chain of logic in this proposition is described concisely by Hemming and Mansoor (1988):

> Property rights (or agency) theory suggests that, because they do not have access to shared information, governments (the principals) face difficulties in providing appropriate incentives to public sector managers (their agents) and in monitoring their performance. Managers are therefore given

less discretion than their private sector counterparts and so
choose a relatively quiet life. . . . They will perform only to
the level necessary to meet the performance standards set for
them, and these may be modest compared with the potential
of the firm or industry concerned. (p. 5)

The logical conclusion, according to property rights scholarship, is
that "private provision of public infrastructure and service would be
more efficient" (Hanke, 1985, p. 14).

*Market Theory*

"Orthodox economic theory of markets" (Buchanan & Tullock,
1962, p. 17) and accompanying perspectives on monopolistic behavior, with their dual engines of competition and profit incentives,
provide the second economic touchstone of privatization advocates.
Indeed, it is safe to say that competition is the "nuclear centre of the
whole privatization argument" (Hardin, 1989, p. 11). That is, "the
more important factor in determining performance may be competition rather than the type of ownership *per se*" (Vickers & Yarrow,
1988, p. 41).

The real issue is not so much public versus private; it is
monopoly versus competition. Far too many government
services—federal, state, and local—are provided as monopolies when they need not be, and it is very difficult to tame
monopolies and make them work in the public interest. So
the introduction of competition is appropriate whether the
competition comes about from the use of vouchers, competitive bidding for service contracts, franchising, or voluntary
efforts. It is the introduction of competition that makes the
difference. (Savas, 1985, p. 23)

Thus, the market theory broadside on public sector services
focuses on the monopolistic nature of that activity: "the underlying,
structural problem of government monopoly . . . is the dominant
factor responsible for malperformance of government services"
(Savas, 1987, p. 251); "the monopolistic nature of local-service delivery is the greatest impediment to government effectiveness" (Bailey,
1991, p. 233). Reviewers maintain that public monopolies "induce
inefficiencies" (Hilke, 1992, p. 134) and "result in the provision of

goods and services substantially lower in quality and higher in cost than those provided in the presence of competition" (Wilson, 1990, p. 65).

According to public choice theorists, these conditions occur because "management policy in government exhibits few of the pressures produced by competition of the profit motive" (Fitzgerald, 1988, pp. 17-18), either for organizations in the way they conduct business or for individuals in the way they acquire information with which to make choices (Tullock, 1988, 1994a). Most troublesome, according to public choice theorists, is the fact that public monopolies "attenuat[e] incentives to minimize costs among managers of government agencies" (Hilke, 1992, p. 134). Because of the absence of competition and profit incentives—the dual engines of markets—public organizations "tend to absorb resources on internal preference scales" (Bailey, 1987, p. 141). This, so our public choice colleagues tell us, fosters "a redirection of production factors towards political rather than economic ends" (Pirie, 1988, p. 5) as well as the evolution of a producer-oriented system "serving the values and meeting the needs of those who direct it and work within it" (p. 7).

> For this reason, no matter how noble the intentions of public employees, no matter how skilled or energetic their efforts, they usually find themselves unable to transcend their bureaucratic restraints to achieve policy goals in a timely, cost-effective manner. (Fitzgerald, 1988, p. 18)

What this means is that "the internal organization is subject to subversion by the bureaucratic process" (Hirsch, 1991, p. 60). The bottom line effect, according to Tullock (1988), is that "the government is apt to impose social costs rather than to eliminate them" (p. 93).

The logical conclusion of this line of reasoning is that markets are to be preferred to government activity—"competition works much better than monopoly [and] a profit incentive is a stronger incentive than any bureaucratic management incentive" (Poole, 1985, p. 37). Competition produces "incentives for improvements in performance" (Hilke, 1992, p. 20) and "tends to motivate organizations to lower prices and sometimes to improve quality" (Brown, 1991, p. 273). "Output which [can] be described as desirable from the standpoint of almost everyone's preference function" (Tullock, 1994b, p. 66) results, and overall economic efficiency is enhanced.

### Political Dimension

> The central insight of the literature now described as public
> choice is that the provision of government services is an
> incidental effect of the incentives and constraints of voters,
> politicians, and bureaucrats. (Niskanen, 1994, p. 270)

> Real governments . . . have decision processes and these de-
> cision processes depend on men who are not only fallible,
> they are also—like the rest of us—more interested in their
> own well-being than that of others. (Tullock, 1994b, p. 68)

> The beneficiaries of government monopoly are politi-
> cians, bureaucrats, and special interest groups. (Bennett &
> DiLorenzo, 1987, p. 22)

One way to frame the political dimension is to revisit Niskanen's
(1971) proposition that public choice theory is concerned with "the
political economy of bureaucracy and representative government"
(p. 12). Viewing the situation with this lens, the public choice literature, critics contend, portrays the public arena as little more than "a
political marketplace where politicians, public employees, and competing groups of beneficiaries seek their narrow interests at the
expense of the general welfare" (Starr, 1987, p. 127). We examine the
interests of each of these three groups below.

### Politicians

Public choice analysts maintain that "the behavior of both the
executive and the legislature can best be interpreted as the result of
maximizing their own personal interests" (Niskanen, 1971, p. 137)—
"that decisions are taken with a view of maximizing the probability
of electoral success" (Vickers & Yarrow, 1988, p. 30). Thus, politicians
are said to employ a type of economic algorithm that closely links
position-taking and election calculations (Stiglitz, 1986): "politicians,
instead of doing what they thought was in the public interest, would
do things which might help them get re-elected, or in some cases,
might raise their income" (Tullock, 1994b, p. 65). In short, "politicians
act in ways that will advance their careers" (Tullock, 1965, p. 29).

The logical deduction here, public choice scholars maintain, is that politicians use tax dollars to enhance their own utility by nurturing the support of the other two players in the public choice triangle—public employees and beneficiaries of governmental programs (Bennett & DiLorenzo, 1987; Niskanen, 1971, 1994). Politicians engage in this tax-funded politics in two main ways: (a) through the creation of programs and the maintenance of existing programs (Pirie, 1988; Tullock, 1965), and (b) through "payoffs to workers in publicly owned firms" (Vickers & Yarrow, 1988, p. 31) in terms of wages, benefits, and job security (Bennett & Johnson, 1980; Savas, 1982). Niskanen (1994) argues that most of this tax-funded self-promotion centers on the portion of a bureau's discretionary budget that the legislature reclaims for its own use through bargaining with the bureau's managers:

> An interesting aspect of the bargaining between a bureau and its political sponsor concerns the distribution of this surplus (the discretionary budget) between spending that serves the interests of the bureaucrats as opposed to the interests of the political review agents. The distribution of this surplus . . . is not determinate. The political review agents exercise their authority . . . as a means to capture some part of the discretionary budget to serve their own special interests (such as the relative use of factor inputs and the geographic distribution of employment and contracts). (p. 274)

In effect, Niskanen argues that the political share of a bureau's surplus (or discretionary budget) provides a system of spoils that allows politicians to "reward their supporters and finance their re-election" (p. 278).

### Bureaucrats

At the heart of the public choice scholarship that provides the theoretical foundation for the privatization movement is a reassessment of the interests of public employees, especially managerial employees well known to us all as government bureaucrats. Central to this reinterpretation is a dismantling or "undermining of the naive faith in the benevolence of governmental bureaucracy" (Buchanan,

1987, p. 206). According to Niskanen (1971), "the beginning of wisdom is the recognition that bureaucrats are people who are, at least, not entirely motivated by the general welfare or the interests of the state" (p. 36). Rather than accepting the assumption that managers of public agencies are "passive agents [who] merely administer and carry out programs" (Bennett & DiLorenzo, 1987, p. 16) with the sole intent of maximizing public interest, public choice analysts advance the belief that these "civil servants often [make] decisions in the interest of their own power or income" (Tullock, 1994b, p. 65): Bureaucrats are much like other people, "people who are less interested in the ostensible objectives of the organization than in their own personal well being" (Tullock, 1965, p. 21)—a well-being that is often expressed in terms of "salary, perquisites, rank, prestige, [and] opportunities for promotion" (Bennett & DiLorenzo, 1987, p. 17).

In economic terms, this means "that government employees, like other economic agents, respond to the opportunities for gain provided by the structure of property rights embedded in the institutions used to control their choices" (De Alessi, 1987, p. 24), and that bureaus act as "a type of special interest group" (Hilke, 1992, p. 13). At the most basic level, this results in the notion of the bureaucrat as a public service maximizer giving way to the conception of a manager who attempts to maximize his or her own utility function—a utility function that contains a variety of variables: "salary, perquisites of the office, public reputation, power, patronage, [and] output of the bureau" (Niskanen, 1971, p. 38). "The two most commonly cited variables that are likely to affect utility in this case are the size of the relevant government department or subdepartment and rents accruing to the officials" (Vickers & Yarrow, 1988, p. 32).

Because, such an analysis continues, improving one's utility function is directly dependent on the resources available to the bureau, budget maximization becomes the operant goal of bureau managers (Niskanen, 1971). Or, more precisely, the objective is to maximize the bureau's discretionary budget (the difference between the total budget and the minimum cost of producing expected outcomes) (Niskanen, 1994). Consequently, managers have a strong incentive to engage in "bureaucratic imperialism" (Tullock, 1965, p. 134) or "empire building" (Dudek & Company, 1989, p. 49). "If such a system is applied throughout a whole organization . . . the higher officials will actually encourage their inferiors to build up the size of the whole hierarchy since their own position, as well as that of their inferiors, will depend on the number of subordinates" (Tullock, 1965, p. 135).

Chapter 3 outlined how the dynamics of maximizing utility and budgets—the fact that "budget expansion benefits bureaucrats" (Hanke, 1989, p. 197)—make "bureaucracy . . . a plausible candidate as an independent source of the growth of government" (Mueller, 1989, p. 338). Here we unpack the logic of the public choice literature, which reveals that budget maximization and empire building impose real costs on citizens in terms of public control and overall efficiency of the economy (Bennett & Johnson, 1980). The switch from maximizing the public interest to maximizing the discretionary budget means that bureaus have the potential to become "producer-oriented" (Pirie, 1988, p. 26), to capture the agency and to direct its energies toward meeting the needs of government employees (Hardin, 1989; Vickers & Yarrow, 1988). The result is goal displacement (Downs, 1967; Tullock, 1965): "Some public sector activities clearly are serving the interest of their own workforce more than the interests of their customers" (Pirie, 1988, p. 26).

The dynamic of provider capture is supported by a number of related conditions. To begin with, bureaus often dominate the relationship with their political sponsors. As Niskanen (1971) reports, "although the nominal relationship of a bureau and its sponsor is that of a bilateral monopoly, the relative incentives and available information, under most conditions, give the bureau the overwhelmingly dominant monopoly power" (p. 30). And even when this is not the case, bureaus still maintain a major role in the bargaining relationship (Niskanen, 1994). Both conditions indicate

> that the political forces which operate within and through the state sector of the economy are more powerful than the forces which government can bring to bear upon it. In the struggle for control, it is more often the government which loses and the institutions of the public sector which win. (Pirie, 1988, p. 49)

Second, even a "bureaucrat who may not be personally motivated to maximize the budget of his bureau is usually driven by conditions both internal and external to the bureau to do just that" (Niskanen, 1971, p. 39). In these cases, budget maximization may be less a "property of rational behavior" (p. 41) than a need to survive in office by meeting the needs—"effective demands" (Niskanen, 1994, p. 272)—of others, especially the bureau's sponsor and employees (Niskanen, 1971, 1994).

Whatever the causes, because (a) "people are more prodigal with the wealth of others than with their own" (Hanke, 1985, p. 6), (b) "public employees have no direct interest in the commercial outcome" (p. 6) of the enterprise, and (c) "the supply of government services by bureaus generates a net surplus that is shared with members of the government" (Niskanen, 1994, p. 278), public choice theory posits that bureaus are characterized by significant inefficiencies (Hilke, 1992; Niskanen, 1971, 1994; Pack, 1991). A cardinal conclusion of public choice scholarship is that "the budget of a bureau is too large, the output . . . may be too low, and the production of this output is uniformly inefficient" (Niskanen, 1994, p. 274); or, more succinctly, "inefficiency in production is the normal condition" (p. 274).

### Employees

It is important to note that in the public choice literature, the motivation and behavior of government employees are viewed as paralleling the interests and actions of their managers: "The employees' interests in larger budgets are obvious and similar to that of the bureaucrat: greater opportunities for promotion, more job security, etc." (Niskanen, 1971, p. 40). Therefore, because "they benefit from continued operation of the public agencies that employ them . . . [they] thus have a vested interest in maintaining public agencies even when they might not be efficient" (Hirsch, 1991, p. 72). More to the point, it is generally in their interests to have an expanding public sector.

One avenue of public choice discourse suggests that because public employees are, next to transfer payment recipients, "the most direct beneficiaries of government spending" (Savas, 1987, p. 26), they are likely to use the power of the ballot box to promote the objective of government growth (Tullock, 1994a): "Government employees have a vested interest in the growth of government and, because of this interest, are very active politically. Relative to the general public, they vote in greater proportion and have a correspondingly disproportionate impact on political decisions" (Bennett & Johnson, 1980, p. 372).

A second plank in the public choice framework holds that public sector unions in particular are key instruments in the growth of bureaus and the concomitant subordination of consumer interests to the objectives of the employees themselves. Ramsey (1987) concludes that, when the economic influence of unions is combined with political muscle, public sector unions have considerable "ability to tax the rest of society" (p. 97).

A final slice of the public choice literature focusing on public employees asserts that employee self-interest is nurtured in what might, presented in the best light, be thought of as a symbiotic relationship with the bureau's sponsor—the intersection where "the self interest of the politician [and] a well-organized union cadre" (p. 97) converge to maximize the utility of both groups:

> The political power of public employees and their unions is not restricted to their voting strength. Political campaign contributors and campaign workers are a potent influence on office seekers. The situation lends itself to collusion whereby officeholders can award substantial pay raises to employees with the unspoken understanding that some of the bread cast upon those particular waters will return as contributions. (Savas, 1987, p. 26)

As described above, the well-being of politicians and government employees often comes at the expense of the general citizenry, especially in inefficiencies visible in inappropriate production schedules and unearned rents enjoyed by public servants (Hilke, 1992; Hirsch, 1991; Niskanen, 1971, 1994).

*Beneficiaries*

If politicians occupy one point on the public choice triangle and employees (bureaucrats and their subordinates) hold down a second, the third is populated by two related groups that also benefit heavily from government sector expenditures—producers and recipients of specific public services. On the issue of service providers as beneficiaries, Bennett and DiLorenzo (1987) and De Hoog (1984) demonstrate that both politicians and bureaucrats mobilize considerable support for themselves by forging strong relationships with private sector producers. Concomitantly, "service providers . . . can become powerful advocates for government spending" (Butler, 1987, p. 6): "Within the business sector, groups develop that see their interests joined to those of the political bureaucracy" (Meltzer & Scott, 1978, p. 116).

At the same time, recipients of public services often act as interest groups that "seek to socialize the costs of services that disproportionately benefit them" (Fixler, 1991, p. 44). At the core of this line of reasoning is the proposition that, because "groups who, one way or another, get the government to provide services for them normally do not pay the full cost, . . . they take advantage of the possibility of imposing part of the cost on other people" (Tullock, 1994b, p. 67). Or, stated less charitably, "interest groups compete in the voting marketplace to redistribute for themselves income plundered through taxation of others" (Fitzgerald, 1988, p. 9). "Well-entrenched private interests . . . succeed in benefiting at the public expense" (Pack, 1991, p. 290).

The public choice literature posits three conditions that make possible these "opportunities for exploitation of the majority by well-organized minorities" (Ross, 1988, p. 14)—what De Alessi (1987) refers to as "wealth redistribution" (p. 29). The first condition is the separation of the beneficiaries from the funders of public services (Ross, 1988). The second is the fact that whereas benefits for any particular interest group "are visible and individual . . . the costs are diffuse and shared by all" (Savas, 1987, p. 20). The third is the presence of a political process that provides a robust vehicle for recipient interest groups to socialize the costs of the benefits accruing to them (Butler, 1987; Meltzer & Scott, 1978; Niskanen, 1994). As is the case with politicians and government employees, producer and recipient interest group self-interest generally results in the situation in which "the amount of service generated is not optimal" (Tullock, 1994b, p. 67), real external costs are imposed (Buchanan & Tullock, 1962), and inefficiencies abound (Niskanen, 1971, 1994; Stiglitz, 1986).

Although public choice theory provides much of the intellectual scaffolding upon which the privatization edifice is built, it remains in the background in a good deal of the privatization literature. The foreground of the picture is often filled with portraits of the benefits that are expected to materialize when services historically housed in the government sector of the economy are transferred to the private sector. We turn our attention to this more practical rationale in the remainder of this chapter.

## Expected Benefits

> Many of these services, as well as commercial services that the government decides to produce for some other reason, can benefit from competition in their production. The potential benefits include substantially lower production costs, improved quality, and enhanced innovation. (Hilke, 1992, p. 136)

> However, the new wave of privatization opportunities does not lend itself to an exclusive focus on cost containment. Where human services are involved, other values—equity, quality, accountability, legitimacy—come into play. (Gormley, 1991a, p. 10)

> The central threat of privatization as the panacea it has become rather than the scalpel it could be is that it abandons to the global market and the powerful forces manipulating it the roles of society and state in shaping the future welfare of citizens. (Martin, 1993, p. 147)

Advocates for privatization maintain that the benefits expected from greater reliance on the marketplace are quite extensive, ranging from cost containment and enhanced efficiency to greater accountability. Opponents, on the other hand, are quick to call into question the putative achievements of privatization—and even when begrudgingly acknowledging gains likely to accrue from market-based reforms, they are apt to couple such recognition with a thorough analysis of the costs of privatization. Thus, for example,

> where advocates of privatization see allocative inefficiency (i.e. government providing services better left to the private sector entirely or provided in too great a quantity, as a result of subsidies, for example), opponents see valued public outputs that would not be forthcoming from the private sector or would not be produced in sufficient quantities. (Pack, 1991, p. 284)

"Conservatives in general and business in particular tend to offer eloquent claims of its virtues. Liberals in general and labor in particular tend to point to its shortcomings and dangers" (Hirsch, 1991, p. 5). Where advocates see gains in productive efficiency and cost savings, opponents discern efforts to "limit both public social spending and the scope of public responsibility" (Ismael, 1988, p. 5).

When entering into this mine field, it is useful to restate the starting point and objective. Although we are not averse to weighing evidence and making judgments about the likely impact of privatization on an array of important outcomes—and, in fact, do some of that work below—it is not our intention to provide an empirical scoreboard on privatization in the various sectors of government. Our prime objective is to unpack and scrutinize the logic in action embedded in the privatization literature in order to assist others in evaluating privatization initiatives in education—to enrich what is often an "impoverished debate" (Martin, 1993, p. 147) rather than to perpetuate the less than fruitful discussions about whether public or private delivery is best (Martin, 1993). We start neither with the belief that privatization will significantly enhance the educational enterprise nor with the assumption that it will wreak havoc on the schooling industry. Rather, we concur with B. W. Brown (1992) that "whether privatization will turn out to be in society's interest must rest . . . on an examination of the production setting in the light of consumers' objectives, and their ability to evaluate output" (p. 293). At the same time, here and throughout the volume, we ground our work on the understanding "that the rational application of any policy instrument is fundamentally a political rather than a technical issue—informed by a whole background of cultural history, public policy goals and resource realities" (Martin, 1993, p. 184). We also contend that a variety of outcome frames (e.g., responsiveness, efficiency, equity, and so forth) are needed to form a robust picture of the logic in action of privatization (Ross, 1988). We continue the portrait we began in Chapter 1, therefore, by examining the panoply of privatization benefits and costs culled from the theoretical and applied literature on the application of privatization in public sectors other than schooling. We focus in particular on four bundles of benefits and costs: efficiency, quality, effects on employees, and values. Our goal, again, is to provide policymakers and educators of all types with an analysis that will help them think more clearly about the application of privatization initiatives to education, especially applications in the service of school improvement.

## Efficiency

> The case for privatization rests primarily, though not exclusively, on the proposition that privatization promotes economic efficiency. (Gormley, 1991b, p. 307)

> If reducing the size of the public sector is the dominant theme in the work of privatization advocates, enhancing the efficiency of the economy as a whole and the public sector in particular is their *leitmotif*. (Pack, 1991, p. 287)

> Of the factors playing a part in privatization discussions, efficiency, often equated with cost, almost always takes center stage. (Hirsch, 1991, p. 76)

Without question, there is one "clear unifying thread" (Bailey, 1991, p. 236) in all the uses of privatization: "maximization of efficiency" (p. 236). Or, as Hula (1990b) remarks, "The search for . . . market efficiency provides perhaps the most common justification for using markets in policy implementation" (p. 13). The basic logic here—"breakdowns rooted in the conflicting interests of principals and agents" (Donahue, 1989, p. 90) analyzed by public choice scholars —has already been explicated. In short, critics argue, because of the "weaknesses inherent in public sector organizations" (Pirie, 1988, p. 38) that we outlined earlier—especially monopolistic structures, political gamesmanship, and bureaucratic self-interest (B. W. Brown, 1992; Hemming & Mansoor, 1988), "political control of a firm leads to gross economic inefficiency" (Ramsey, 1987, p. 98). "The above problems suggest that public enterprises will perform badly in terms of productive efficiency, because they are likely to have higher production costs at a given level of output than comparable enterprises in the private sector" (Hemming & Mansoor, 1988, p. 5). One result of this is that "potential efficiency gains [in the public sector] are allegedly substantial" (Pack, 1991, p. 286). Another is that increasing competition via privatization strategies "can both directly improve efficiency and reduce the total costs of government service"

(Hilke, 1992, p. 7) "while improving or at least maintaining the level and quality of public services" (Savas, 1987, p. 6).

> Governments in the United States spend roughly half a trillion dollars per year paying public workers to deliver goods and services directly. If only one-quarter of this total turned out to be suitable for privatization, at an average savings of, say, 25 percent—and neither figure is recklessly optimistic—the public would save over $30 billion. The prospects of government spending that much less, or of being able to *do* that much more, should appeal to Americans of whatever political leanings. (Donahue, 1989, p. 216)

*Cost Issues*

*Cost Containment.* At the most basic level in the privatization literature, efficiency equates (inappropriately) with cost savings (Hirsch, 1991): "The principal argument for privatization is that government-run programs are more costly than privately-managed programs" (Van Horn, 1991, p. 271), and the "anticipation of reduced costs of public services is the most compelling reason for both scholars and government officials to favor contracting out" (De Hoog, 1984, p. 6) and other forms of privatization (B. W. Brown, 1992; Gormley, 1991b; Hilke, 1992; Moore, 1987). Because "it is assumed that the private sector can produce goods at lower unit costs than the public sector" (Hula, 1990b, p. 7), "privatization ultimately is supposed to serve as a cost saving proposition" (Fitzgerald et al., 1990, p. 71) that improves government performance in the public interest (Pack, 1991).

What do we know about the viability of the cost savings argument that undergirds privatization? To begin with, although there is some skepticism on the issue (which we examine below), the following assessment by Darr (1991) appears valid: "The majority of experts would appear to agree that real financial savings are frequently possible, although they are neither automatic nor easily achieved" (p. 68). The collective data on cost containment and cost savings reinforce this expert judgment: "The privatization of individual public services frequently results in significantly lower costs" (Clarkson, 1989, p. 157). Indeed, "extensive research on privatization has revealed that private firms are almost always far more efficient than government enterprises in providing a wide array of services" (Bennett & DiLorenzo, 1987, p. 14). Although it is difficult to aggregate studies across the various domains of privatization, three summative conclusions can be drawn. First, as noted earlier, opportunities for cost savings from privatization loom large (Clarkson, 1989; Donahue, 1989; Hilke, 1992; President's Commission on Privatization, 1988); second, privatization can help municipalities avoid or spread out large-scale capital expenditures (Roehm et al., 1991; Savas, 1987); and third, providing services by private firms in a competitive environment saves taxpayers between 15% and 40% over the cost of providing them publicly (Bennett & Johnson, 1980; Clarkson, 1989; Dudek & Company, 1989; Moore, 1987; Pirie, 1985).

*Cautions.* Because influences are afoot that sometimes overstate and sometimes undervalue potential cost savings from privatization, reformers would be advised to approach potential cost savings in education with caution, especially as privatization initiatives move from the more peripheral domains of schooling (e.g., transportation) to the core program. We review the most important of these forces below under the headings of nonviability of cost savings, methodological issues, and differences between cost and efficiency.

Much of the work in this area consists of one-time, cross-sectional analyses. This is noteworthy because, for a variety of reasons, there is some concern that cost savings from privatization may diminish over time (De Hoog, 1984; Pack, 1991); that is, that "initial savings are not indicative of longer term outcomes" (Pack, 1991, p. 301). Thus, "caution and the test of time are warranted in the area of cost comparisons" (Committee on the Judiciary, 1986, p. 124). Scholars hypothesize that this *nonviability of cost savings* can be traced to at least four factors: a deterioration of the competitive environment, an increase in government regulations, postcontractual opportunistic behavior on the part of contractors, and the generation of new spending coalitions. On the first issue, investigators such as De Hoog (1984) and Pack (1991) reveal that savings from privatization may decrease or disappear over time as there is an "evolution of the system from one explicitly designed to promote competition among private contractors to one that substantially inhibits competition" (Pack, 1991, p. 302). One problem is that "competition is costly" (Donahue, 1989, p. 126), and the energy needed to maintain it through contracting and monitoring often tends to diminish. Another difficulty is that, over time, "governments may become captive of particular contractors" (Starr, 1991, p. 31)—a condition that is likely to occur where there is a limited number of suppliers (Ascher, 1991; Peters, 1991) and where the government agency is the sole purchaser of services. Thus, "primarily due to the lack of responsive and responsible suppliers and the lack of desire or resources by officials to create competitive procedures" (De Hoog, 1984, p. 54), competition may be much less robust under privatization than "traditional economic doctrine about competition" (De Hoog, 1984, p. 54) assumes. One possible consequence "is that the growth of privatization may ultimately lead to a shift from public-service monopolies to private-service monopolies" (Darr, 1991, p. 65). "As a result, the contractors may be able to raise prices dramatically, and the initial advantages of contracting out may vanish like a mirage" (Starr, 1991, p. 31).

The competitive environment may also weaken for other reasons. One of the most devastating and disheartening of these is corruption (Brown, 1991; Hatry, 1991; Kolderie, 1991; Thayer, 1987; Van Horn, 1991). Indeed, Hanke (1989) hypothesizes that "possibly the most potent factor limiting the spread of privatization is the specter of corruption" (p. 202)—payoffs that "reduce the quality of goods or services actually delivered" (Thayer, 1987, p. 152) and "prevent [the] firm from doing an efficient job" (p. 147). A second cause for the weakening of the competitive environment—what has been labeled "cooptative politics" by De Hoog (1984, p. 28)—focuses on the evolution of a new type of interest group politics—one now shaped less by government employees and more by "contractor contributions to political campaigns" (Van Horn, 1991, p. 274) and the benefits of mutual relationships between bureaucrats, legislators, and contractors (De Hoog, 1984). A third cause might best be labeled the publicization of the private sector, or what Starr (1987) refers to as "the socialization of private provision" (p. 130). That is, at a minimum, "privatization will invite greater regulation of the private sector, ultimately making the private sector less distinctive than it is today" (Gormley, 1991a, p. 12). More dramatically, it is suggested that "rather than fostering the debureaucratization . . . that is the essence of the privatization vision, it is more likely that these noxious features of the welfare state will devolve unto the private sector" (Ismael, 1988, p. 6).

Closely related to this last issue—the infection of markets with the inherent deficiencies of public delivery rather than the marketization of the public sector—is the belief that privatization, especially in human services fields, will be accompanied by significant increases in government regulations (Gormley, 1991b). According to Pack (1991), the likelihood of this eventuality is most pronounced for "personal services for which the production process is critical" (p. 303)—a condition that clearly characterizes the education industry. Pack goes on to suggest that "increased regulation has several important consequences: it encumbers, it reduces flexibility in providing services in innovative ways, and it increases administrative costs. As a result, it inhibits precisely those outcomes that private providers seek" (p. 302). She concludes that "sufficiently stringent regulation may make private provision nearly indistinguishable" (p. 282) from public production.

Cost-saving benefits also can be eliminated over time by what Hirsch (1991) refers to as "postcontractual opportunistic behavior" (p. 91). The starting point in this argument has been laid out nicely by Fitzgerald et al. (1990): "The acid test of returning to oversight through privatization is the degree to which contractors fall under any real scrutiny" (p. 71). Postcontractual opportunistic behavior undermines the integrity of the contracting process and the monitoring function. Ironically, it begins at the start of the contracting process, when bidders engage in "low-balling" (Fixler & Poole, 1987, p. 172) tactics—"offer[ing] low prices in order to win contracts and then increas[ing] prices once their relationship with the agency has been established" (Pack, 1991, p. 300). "The objective is to win the job and then extract higher rates from the government once the opportunity to switch contractors has passed" (Worsnop, 1992, p. 981). Contract manipulation continues after an agreement has been secured through attempts to "take advantage of contract clauses or informal understandings that allow adjustments that will reduce costs, reduce output quality, or increase payments" (Hirsch, 1991, p. 91).

Finally, expected cost savings may fail to materialize or may be lost over time because privatization, especially contracting out, can "create a powerful prospending constituency" (Moore, 1987, p. 69)—"a vested interest in favor of continued government spending [in] the private sector" (Gormley, 1991b, p. 312)—so that "contracting out public services to private interests often ends up costing taxpayers more, not less" (Worsnop, 1992, p. 984). According to Starr (1991), this may occur because, "rather than being dependent on the market, the private firms receiving contracts and vouchers will still be dependent on public appropriations, and they have every reason to try to milk the public treasury for all it is worth" (p. 30)—not unlike the special interest groups at work in Chapter 4 under public provision. As Kolderie (1991) notes, "Moving the supply (producer) function out of government may replace a muted bureaucratic pressure for bigger programs with a well-financed, private-sector campaign" (p. 256) (see also De Hoog, 1984; Hula, 1990b; Pack, 1991), the outcome of which is "an alliance between private sector suppliers and government officials at the taxpayers' expense" (Donahue, 1989, p. 128).

*Methodological issues* concerning studies that examine costs are of some concern. To begin with, "There are large differences of realized savings . . . [and] there are disparities in the estimates of potential savings" (Pack, 1991, p. 297). A good deal of judgment is involved in the science of calculating the cost advantages of privatization. Some analysts contend, for example, that conclusions are based on "heroically selective attention" (Starr, cited in Worsnop, 1992, p. 993) on the part of reviewers. They note in particular the tendency to overlook nonconfirming evidence. The writings of other reviewers also remind us that speculative analysis and anecdotal reporting often characterize the literature on privatization's cost benefits.

Because of the problematic nature of cost comparisons—the "difficulty in identifying and measuring all of the costs associated with each service delivery alternative" (De Hoog, 1984, p. 9)—cost measurements in privatization studies often leave a good deal of room for improvement (Peters, 1991; Pirie, 1988). On one hand, because "the costs of public sector operations are often very difficult to calculate" (Pirie, 1988, p. 21) (see also Ascher, 1991; Kolderie & Hauer, 1991), the full costs of services provided in the public sector are often understated, thus "bias[ing] cost comparisons in favor of the municipality" (Bennett & Johnson, 1980, p. 376) and generally undervaluing the savings benefits of privatization initiatives (Darr, 1991):

> Promarket analysts . . . have suggested that the advantages
> of private supply would be clearer if comparisons included

equipment maintenance, capital expenditures, the full fringe
benefit packages (including future pensions) of municipal
workers, etc.—items that are not usually included in municipal service budgets by service areas. James T. Bennett and
Manuel H. Johnson argue that adding the opportunity costs
of public production would also widen the cost differences
in favor of private production. (De Hoog, 1984, p. 9)

Indeed, the results from one study suggest that "the true cost of a
government service, measured properly using valid cost-accounting
procedures, was 30 percent greater than the cost nominally ascribed
to that service in the formal budget" (Savas, 1987, p. 259).

Tax benefits (and costs) in particular often complicate cost analysis. Their treatment—especially the tendency to overlook them—is
"the source of many errors" (Savas, 1987, p. 26) in the privatization
literature. Yet their "explicit recognition . . . is important in identifying the necessary cost condition for a temporary privatization step"
(Hirsch, 1991, p. 104). The problem stems from the fact that the
government does not pay taxes—"public production has a cost advantage over private production" (p. 104). Private firms, on the other
hand, "pay many taxes and fees that government agencies do not"
(Savas, 1987, p. 261): "Once a specific service is privatized and is
provided by a private firm, which unlike the public agency pays
taxes, a variety of governments receive additional tax revenue"
(Hirsch, 1991, p. 121). Thus, the transfer of production from the
public to the private sector produces "additional government revenues which are currently forgone" (Bennett & Johnson, 1980, p. 393).
The cost issue here, as both Savas (1987) and Hirsch (1991) remind
us, is that "taxes and fees paid by a contractor to all government units
constitute a rebate to the public and should properly be subtracted
from his price in order to arrive at a figure that can be compared
correctly with the cost of the government service" (Savas, 1987,
p. 261). Because such calculations are not the norm, the cost of public
provision is understated (Dudek & Company, 1989), and there is less
privatization than there should be (Hirsch, 1991).

Hidden or unspecified expenses can cut both ways, however.
That is, they can understate the real costs of privatization as well as
of public provision. The primary cost of privatization that is often
"overlooked is the government's administrative costs of determining

procedures and awarding, negotiating, writing, and monitoring contracts. These expenditures obviously are not reflected in contract amounts, but for some services (e.g. human services), they are probably substantial" (De Hoog, 1984, p. 9).

> The standard cost of contracts can be classified as follows. In the contract formation stage, the specification of possible contingencies will incur costs: the parties involved have to identify the contingencies and predetermine what the terms should be under such circumstances. In the contract performance stage, monitoring is needed to detect violations of contract terms, and this supervision increases costs. Contract terms must then be enforced, which can add the costs of arbitration, settlement, or going to court. (Hirsch, 1991, pp. 56-57)

These later-stage contract costs—monitoring and enforcement—have been pegged at "from 2 to 7 percent of the contract price" (Savas, 1987, p. 260). "When the firm produces in-house, however, only one 'inspection' is needed. So it seems that a decision in favor of privatization requires that the cost saving from contracting out be greater than the additional inspection cost" (Hirsch, 1991, p. 96).

Two further issues regarding the comparison of cost analyses also deserve attention. The first informs us that caution is in order in assuming that, even when cost advantages of privatization are real, they will transfer to education. The second calls into question the desirability and appropriateness of making cost the prime criterion against which to assess public services. The former line of analysis points out that most of the studies to date have examined privatization in dimensions of the physical environment (De Hoog, 1984; Gormley, 1991a, 1991b). Some analysts question whether findings from these dimensions will hold up when privatization initiatives focus on areas of social and human services, such as education (De Hoog, 1984; Donahue, 1989). For a variety of reasons—the human intensity of social services coupled with a lack of potential for cost savings from technology, "the need for the government to specify closely and oversee the delivery of such sensitive services" (Pack, 1991, p. 302), the presence of deep moral and ethical issues, and the inherent "inhibition on competition" (p. 302)—these scholars suggest that a change in the locus of production will not be accompanied by substantial change in the incentives for or the constraints on efficiency. Without these, the performances of the private nonprofit organizations may be expected to differ little from that of the public agencies. (p. 302)

Many analysts remind us that cost comparisons often fail to acknowledge the fact that "public enterprises are assigned multiple objectives" (Hemming & Mansoor, 1988, p. 4), especially redistributional and other expensive social goals (Martin, 1993) that public agencies "are directed to pursue or informally adopt" (Hilke, 1992, p. 95)—what Berry and Lowery (1987) refer to as "the full dimension of performance characteristics we might desire in social and economic relationships" (p. 7). "What needs to be emphasized is that the efficient provision of public goods and services is not always intended by legislative bodies when considering the adoption of public policy: this is but one possible objective among others" (Wilson, 1990, p. 63). A number of points follow from the claim that public agencies "embody additional values and goals" (Hilke, 1992, p. 29) "unrelated to economic efficiency" (p. 131). First, "productive efficiency is simply not the cardinal value of civil service organizations" (Donahue, 1989, p. 216) (see also Berry & Lowery, 1987). That is, "other goals adopted by the agency may conflict with the quality and cost goals that private firms would be expected to pursue exclusively" (Hilke, 1992, p. 14). Second, because "the public sector is held to different requirements than the private sector" (Pack, 1991, p. 291)—that is, "public tasks are different" (Donahue, 1989, p. 215)—"cost comparisons are not meaningful" (Pack, 1991, p. 292). Third, if cost comparisons are to be meaningful, these additional "public purposes . . . must be taken into account in considering the relative efficiency of public and private production" (Pack, 1991, p. 292).

Finally, the *difference between cost and efficiency* merits treatment. Specifically, as a number of investigations remind us (De Hoog, 1984; Frug, 1991; Martin, 1993; Ross, 1988), cost savings are not synonymous with enhanced efficiency. "The debate over the cost advantages of privatization also often fails to distinguish between those savings that are net efficiency gains to society as a whole and those that represent transfers from one sector of society to another" (Gomez-Ibanez et al., 1990, p. 144). Privatization proponents are all too "preoccupied with potential cost reductions stemming from privatization. They appear to equate cost reductions with efficiency increases. The two are not necessarily the same" (Hirsch, 1991, p. 124). "It is clearly inappropriate to identify efficiency as any reduction in cost" (Hula, 1990b, p. 14). Lower costs can result from either "greater efficiency or deteriorating quality" (Starr, 1987, p. 129)— from greater productivity or "from reducing the standard of service or by paying lower wages and imposing poorer work conditions on staff" (Bell & Cloke, 1990, p. 12). The goal "is not merely to cut costs but to do so without reducing benefits by a commensurate amount" (Gormley, 1991a, p. 7). "To the extent that cost reductions are achieved by reductions in level and quality of service, claims of increased efficiency are illusionary" (Hula, 1990b, p. 1). Thus, "a finding that private firms have lower unit costs than their public counterparts does not necessarily imply that their contributions to social welfare are greater; questions relating to allocative efficiency and to the quality of goods or services provided also need to be taken into account" (Vickers & Yarrow, 1988, p. 40).

*Issues of Allocative and Productive Efficiency*

> Given that the relative performance of publicly and privately owned firms in respect of allocative and internal efficiency will depend upon a range of factors that includes the effectiveness of the respective monitoring systems, the degree of competition in the market, regulatory policy, and the technological progressiveness of the industry, evaluation of the welfare implications of privatization necessarily depends upon empirical assessment of the role and significance of each of these various factors. (Vickers & Yarrow, 1988, p. 29)

*Definitions.* As we noted earlier, "the principal justification for the private provision of public goods and services is efficiency" (Wilson, 1990, p. 61)—the belief that private firms are more efficient than government agencies in delivering goods and services (Bennett & DiLorenzo, 1987). In short, "privatization is basically an economic efficiency issue" (Seader, 1991, p. 32). At the heart of the efficiency logic undergirding privatization is the belief that because of three inherent sources of inefficiency in public ownership—"political interference and bureaucratic failure" (Hemming & Mansoor, 1988, p. 5) and "monopoly power" (B. W. Brown, 1992, p. 288)—"the public sector . . . is virtually by definition an inferior vehicle for pursuing economic activity" (Berry & Lowery, 1987, p. 5). The core tenet is that the private sector outperforms government by (a) ensuring that the goods and services desired by consumers are the ones actually provided and (b) producing the same levels of outcome at lower costs (Bennett & Johnson, 1980; Hemming & Mansoor, 1988).

Efficiency is thus about two primary issues—how goods and services are allocated, or the mix of goods and services provided, and how goods and services are produced. The first point is concerned with "the price efficiency of optional resource allocation" (Hirsch, 1991, p. 76) and is known as *allocative efficiency*. The second issue focuses on "the input-output production transformation" (p. 76) and is known as productive efficiency. Allocative inefficiency can be traced to the monopoly status of many public agencies:

> While public ownership per se may lead to productive inefficiency, it can result in allocative inefficiency only when associated with considerable monopoly power—which is often granted by statute—or when some other form of protection from competitive pressures—usually the result of inappropriate financial and trade policies—is implied. (Hemming & Mansoor, 1988, p. 5)

Allocative inefficiency occurs when agencies "fail to allocate . . . assets to their best and highest uses" (Thompson, 1989, p. 205)—when "prices are artificially high" (Hilke, 1992, p. 139). The result is that agencies "produce the wrong mix of services, or even do not produce some valued programs at all" (B. W. Brown, 1992, p. 288)—"the quantity, quality, and other characteristics of goods and services are not those most valued by consumers" (Hemming & Mansoor, 1988, p. 5).

Productive inefficiency, on the other hand, "occurs when more inputs (labor, raw materials, energy, etc.) are used than necessary" (Hilke, 1992, p. 139). Unlike allocative inefficiency, it can be traced to all three sources of inefficiency listed earlier—monopoly status, bureaucratic failure, and political interference. Productive efficiency, in turn, is often divided into technical and organizational efficiency:

Technical efficiency involves the availability of choice concerning the appropriate production function and combination of inputs, that is, to what extent cost can be minimized given quality and quantity constraints. . . . Organizational efficiency concerns the question of whether the appropriate production technology is actually known and utilized by decision makers in a manner that maximizes output, given the level of inputs and their prices, and/or minimizes costs for given levels of outputs. Therefore it is mainly concerned with the internal organization of the entity producing the good. (Hirsch, 1991, pp. 67-68)

*The Logic of Efficiency.* Efficiency benefits that are attributed to privatization are not dependent

on the suggestion that private operators are wiser, kinder, or harder working than people in government service but on the proposition that scarce resources are more likely to be allocated to their most urgent uses if operated by profit-seeking owners than if administered "in the public interest" by political bodies. (Roth, 1987, p. 76)

Also, because public agencies use more capital and labor than private-sector firms for a given level of output, private firms are more efficient than firms owned and operated by government. The rationale for this private sector efficiency has been laid out nicely by Wilson (1990) and Donahue (1989):

- Private ownership allows the concentration of interest in efficiency; public ownership does not. (Donahue, 1989, p. 133)
- Public organizations usually are secure against competition; private organizations frequently are not. (Donahue, 1989, p. 133)
- Service boundaries can be defined on the basis of economic considerations (e.g., economies of scale) rather than historical accident. (Wilson, 1990, p. 61)
- Public management is constrained by layered authority, mandatory reviews, civil service rules, formal bid procedures, and so on; private management is not. (Donahue, 1989, p. 133). Managers of private sector firms have incentives for efficiencies not present in the public sector. (Wilson, 1990, p. 62)

- Private firms that fail to deliver face bankruptcy; public agencies that fail to deliver do not. (Donahue, 1989, p. 133)

We break down this efficiency rationale below into five parts: market incentives, structural productivity, labor productivity, management productivity, and capital productivity.

Nearly everyone involved in discussions on privatization agrees that it is "romantic" (Donahue, 1989, p. 222) to assume that a simple change in ownership—"without competition and without market tests" (Donahue, 1989, p. 222)—will lead to greater efficiency (Donahue, 1989; Hemming & Mansoor, 1988). Indeed, it is widely acknowledged that it is the subjection of the public sector "to the competitive forces of the marketplace and *market incentives*" (Bennett & Johnson, 1980, p. 365, emphasis added)—"the introduction of marketlike competition into public service provision" (De Hoog, 1984, p. 18)—that ensures that the efficiency gains of privatization are realized. Where "competition is absent . . . abuses commonly associated with monopolies are likely to occur" (Hirsch, 1991, p. 83) and "market incentives for efficiency are absent" (Bennett & Johnson, 1980, p. 366).

Privatization, it is argued, leads in turn to increased competition. A "unifying criterion of policymaking" (Bailey, 1987, p. 141) "the free-market profit motive" (Renner, 1989, p. 1)—is loaded into the service provision equation (Moore, 1987; Savas, 1985). Proprietary rights are introduced (Donahue, 1989), and "consumer sovereignty" (Pack, 1991, p. 283) (see also Butler, 1991; Ramsey, 1987) is enhanced. These changes are accompanied by new incentive structures (Bennett & Johnson, 1980; Ross, 1988). "Potent incentives for innovation" (Donahue, 1989, p. 42), in turn, materialize. Because there are "better factor price signals" (Gomez-Ibanez et al., 1990, p. 153), the true costs of production become clearer (De Hoog, 1984). "Competing sellers have strong profit incentives to minimize costs for any given quality and to offer consumers the highest quality for any given price in order to gain and retain customers" (Hilke, 1992, p. 1). The "financial discipline of private capital markets" (Hemming & Mansoor, 1988, p. 6) is brought into the picture.

In summary, this chain of logic provides that, as "a function of the discipline imposed . . . by competition and efforts to maximize profit" (Hula, 1990b, p. 15), government can be improved. The cardinal principle here is that "the economy of private market values" (Bailey, 1987, p. 141)—"the disciplines of competition and the need to earn a profit" (Pirie, 1988, p. 22)—keeps private firms leaner and more efficient than public agencies: "The discipline imposed by the operation of the market system provides inherent incentives for economic efficiency" (Bennett & Johnson, 1980, p. 369).

Private production is also expected to be more *structurally productive* than that of public agencies because of efficiencies that can be garnered through economies of scale (Dudek & Company, 1989; Peters, 1991; Savas, 1987): "Economic theory suggests that private rather than public enterprise should be the more efficient producer of goods and services, since private firms may seek optimal scale of operation without the constraints imposed by political boundaries" (Bennett & Johnson, 1980, p. 392). Or, conversely, "public production of goods and services is inherently inefficient because economies of scale and finance cannot be realized" (Bennett & Johnson, 1980, p. 367). According to the logic of scale economies, "the scale of public firms is not determined by economic criteria, but by the size of the political jurisdiction" (Hirsch, 1991, p. 78), that is, by "historical accidents" (Bennett & Johnson, 1980, p. 365) and "political considerations" (p. 366). As a consequence, municipalities are often either too small to recognize the benefits of scale economies or "so large so as to be confronted with scale diseconomies" (Hirsch, 1991, p. 78). In contrast to public agencies, "the private sector has more flexibility" (Seader, 1991, p. 36). "The private firm may adjust its scale of operations to exploit fully any economies of scale or to avoid any diseconomies which may be present in the provision of a particular good or service" (Bennett & Johnson, 1980, p. 366)—or, as Hirsch (1991) reports, to "adopt a size that is favorable under existing production technologies" (p. 78). In particular, private firms "can spread the costs of capital and overhead across several cities" (Donahue, 1989, p. 141), thus realizing the benefits of "multijurisdiction economics" (Brown, 1991, p. 273) (see also Miller & Tufts, 1991).

At the same time, it is important to acknowledge that public firms may have structural dimensions that can promote efficiency in the production and delivery of goods and services (Gomez-Ibanez et al., 1990). For example, efficiency can result from what Hirsch (1991) describes as "economies of scope" (p. 79), reduced transaction costs (or efficiencies) that result from "circular integration," that is, "when a variety of complementary services are produced under a single government's control and supervision" (p. 79). According to Hirsch, there are two dimensions to these economies of scope:

One relates to the cost of supplying a service and the other to the consumer's costs in receiving a service. Because of the economies of scope, cost savings can be generated by joint supply and the utility of some public goods will increase (consumption costs will fall) if supplied in a coordinated fashion. (p. 79)

More concretely, De Hoog (1984) notes that circular integration and the resultant economies "are realized in some jurisdictions through the reduction of overhead, start-up costs, or high personnel costs by spreading supply over a large number of units or other agencies" (p. 6). Concomitantly, some reviewers maintain that the "limited jurisdictional borders" (Bailey, 1987, p. 143) that define public provision promote economies in service production. According to scholars who put forward this argument, "geographical fragmentation presents an incentive ultimately and, over time, toward efficiency" (p. 143).

There is some evidence that "labour costs are often the key to differences in efficiency between the public and private sectors" (Pirie, 1988, p. 23). There is also considerable support for the claim that privatization is associated with reduced employee costs and increased *labor productivity* (Dudek & Company, 1989)—"a mixture of [1] reduced economic rents in the form of lower rates of compensation and [2] efficiency gains" (Hilke, 1992, p. 132), or "reductions in real resources used in producing . . . services" (Hilke, 1992, p. 119). On the first point, which can be thought of succinctly as the labor cost issue, the case is sometimes made that there are "inherent flaws in government provision" (Fixler, 1991, p. 41) when it comes to labor. To begin with, the principles of the public choice theorists presented earlier suggest that there is "a bias toward labor as an input in bureaucratic operations" (Bennett & Johnson, 1980, p. 388). The interests of bureaucratic managers and agency employees merge to create an overemphasis on the personnel dimension and an underemphasis on the capital aspects of government firms, especially at the local and state levels (Bennett & Johnson, 1980; Pirie, 1985).

Some privatization scholars also maintain that the pervasive use of "legislative directives such as civil service provisions" (Hirsch, 1991, p. 79) or "public personnel controls" (De Hoog, 1984, p. 6) contribute to the inefficiency of public agencies (Dudek & Company, 1989; Fixler, 1991). For example, according to Hilke (1992):

Efficiency within government organizations . . . may be impeded by application of rules and regulations designed to prevent politicalization or corruption of other parts of that government. In sections of the government that provide what many regard as inherently governmental services, such rules may be important. However, the application of these rules to all in-house production may lead to inefficiencies by needlessly raising operating costs. . . . Moving a service from in-house production, where such rules may have to apply, to outside production, where such rules are less necessary and less common, may improve efficiency. (pp. 13-14)

Hirsch (1991) takes us even a step further in his analysis of the inefficiencies embedded in civil service rules associated with public employment:

Civil service provisions provide guidelines intended to eliminate political patronage and to compensate and promote workers according to their productive contributions rather than to political, racial, or other noneconomic factors. Yet, in securing equal treatment for all workers, these guidelines have in recent years tended to inflate wages and retain workers of relatively low quality. The positive aspects of civil service provisions have been overshadowed over the years by abuses and rigidities, often making them counterproductive. Civil service provisions can raise not only total compensation but can also reduce management's flexibility and thereby impede efficiency. (pp. 80, 83)

The final labor cost issue focuses on the collective bargaining process in the public sector (Fitzgerald et al., 1990) and the "compensation premium" (Hilke, 1992, p. 126) or rents enjoyed by "government employees relative to many private sector workers" (p. 126). The central proposition here is that, given the disconnection between the public firm and marketplace incentives, cost savings that should accrue to consumers are equally likely to be advantageous to employees in terms of enhanced wages and benefits, more favorable patterns of work, and/or more lenient work rules. This absence of incentives and profits also means that there is a "tendency [on the part] of municipal management to be more accommodating to its employees, especially in collective bargaining situations, than private sector counterparts" (Fitzgerald et al., 1990, p. 71). Exacerbating all of this is the fact that there is more unionization in the public than in the private sector, resulting in the development of a working environment that often severely restrains management's "flexible use of labour in terms of time and skills" (Pirie, 1988, p. 23). Consequently, in the public sector, the likelihood of employees "acquiring various perquisites that increase production costs is greater than in private firms" (Hanke & Walters, 1987, p. 106). Public managers are thus less able to use labor as efficiently as their public sector colleagues.

Although the reduction of costs through the elimination of compensation premiums or rents is an important dimension of labor productivity, efficient use of labor is the issue of paramount importance. Turning to the employment of labor in the production process, then, we find considerable evidence that "a substantial portion of total cost savings from privatization represents real resource savings" (Hilke, 1992, p. 133)—"reductions in real resources used in producing [a] service" (Hilke, 1992, p. 119) (see also Dudek & Company, 1989). Indeed, Hatry (1991) argues that "perhaps the main virtue of the privatization movement is that it encourages public employees to improve their own productivity in order to help ensure their own competitiveness in the face of privatization" (p. 266)— "that it stimulates impressive in-house productivity improvements" (Dudek & Company, 1989, p. 38). According to this line of thought, "the incentive system in the private sector makes employees more productive than does the system adopted by government" (Frug, 1991, p. 306). Competition inherent in "the private sector encourages *public* employees to be more innovative and to improve public employee efficiency" (Brown, 1991, p. 275). The ability of the private "contractor . . . to use labor more efficiently" (Pirie, 1985, p. 65) means that [he or she] employs fewer workers than the government to perform the same service" (Dudek & Company, 1989, p. 32)—that he or she is able to "complete jobs faster and with fewer employees" (Darr, 1991, p. 64).

*Management productivity* also acts as a key mediating variable between privatization and enhanced efficiency. Although Bailey (1987) cautions that "public management is simply different from private management" (p. 141) and that "the two are not directly comparable" (p. 141), comparisons nevertheless abound in the privatization literature. There are extensive claims that the private sector is characterized by more "management know how" (Van Horn, 1991, p. 262) and "more effective financial management" (Hemming & Mansoor, 1988, p. 12). Privatization advocates assume that, because of "the potential for chronic inefficiency [that] is a special peril for collective endeavors" (Donahue, 1989, p. 51), "private managers can deliver at lower costs services similar or superior to those of public managers" (Bailey, 1987, p. 141).

According to some analysts, one limitation on the efficiency of public managers can be traced to "restrictions on management's decision-making power" (Hirsch, 1991, p. 83). Scholars offer two primary lines of explanation in this area. They believe, as we discussed earlier, that collective bargaining contracts, by "impos[ing] guidelines on personnel practices . . . inhibit the ability of management to utilize efficient production processes" (p. 81). In particular, they discern reduced "flexibility in supervision practices such as hiring and firing workers" (Hilke, 1992, p. 160). These reviewers also suggest that a web of "legislative directives . . . and civil service provisions" (Hirsch, 1991, p. 81), as well as other constraints of public ownership (e.g., restrictions emanating from the press), may unduly confine management decision making (Bailey, 1987; Gomez-Ibanez et al., 1990).

The essence of the management productivity logic, however, focuses on incentive systems, specifically the proposition that

> a vastly different incentive structure exists for the manager of the private firm vis-à-vis the manager of the public firm, and it can be shown that the incentive structure in the public sector hinders rather than enhances the efficient provision of goods and services. (Bennett & Johnson, 1980 p. 366)

The reasoning here, in turn, rests upon foundations we outlined earlier, especially "the attenuation of ownership inherent in public undertakings" (Donahue, 1989, p. 51) and the "lack of exchangeability" (Hirsch, 1991, p. 86) that defines the public sector. Absent ownership and the profit motive, the utility of public managers, it is proposed, depends to some significant extent on the size of the agency's budget—as reflected primarily in terms of the level of employment. Bennett and Johnson (1980) lay out the reasoning here as follows:

> The market imposes a discipline on the manager in the private sector that is absent in the public sector. In contrast to the manager of the private firm whose utility is increased by profit maximization, the self-interest of the manager of a government bureau is enhanced by increasing the number of subordinates. (p. 392)

The result, they maintain, is that "incentives for economic efficiency [are] largely, if not totally, absent" (p. 371) for public sector managers.

Examining the issue from another perspective—not the inefficiency of the bureau, but rather the efficiency of the private firm—some reviewers assert that, "because of differences in economic environments" (Bennett & Johnson, 1980, p. 368), the managers of private firms "face stronger incentives to manage . . . in a cost effective manner" (Hanke & Dowdle, 1987, p. 121); their "incentives for efficiency are vastly different from those in the public sector" (Bennett & Johnson, 1980, p. 368). To begin with, the case holds, "private managers will be spared the various procedural requirements that tend to distract public managers from the pursuit of technical efficiency and mandated practices that (at least in economic terms) are decidedly inferior" (Donahue, 1989, pp. 161-162). Thus, according to Savas (1987), privatization "permits better management, free of most of the distracting influences that are characteristic of overtly political organizations" (p. 109); it allows managers to "make decisions independently of the need to meet the demands of political expediency" (Hemming & Mansoor, 1988, p. 12). More important, bestowing property rights and instilling the profit motive ensure that "the consequences of managerial decisions are borne most directly by the decision maker" (Peters, 1991, p. 58) (see also Hanke & Walters, 1987; Ramsey, 1987). One key product of this linkage is that "in the private sector the self interest of the manager is enhanced by increasing economic efficiency" (Bennett & Johnson, 1980, p. 365); managers in this sphere, as opposed to their public sector colleagues, "can anticipate some degree of personal benefit from increased efficiency" (Donahue, 1989, p. 162). Self-interest here is conceived in terms of both carrots and sticks (Savas, 1987). The former take the shape of "monetary incentives [and] . . . the prospect of advancement into higher posts" (Donahue, 1989, p. 162). The latter are expressed through more vigorous monitoring of managerial performance

(Hanke & Walters, 1987; Hemming & Mansoor, 1988; Hirsch, 1991), termination or demotion (Bennett & Johnson, 1980; Savas, 1987), or "competition from more efficient firms that may eventually drive the firm from the market" (Bennett & Johnson, 1980, p. 366).

Finally, efficiency gains are expected from privatization initiatives because of the potential for more *productive use of capital:*

> One reason the private sector may be perceived to be more efficient in the use of its resources is that there is an internal incentive for managers to lower per unit fixed costs and raise utilization rates of capital, that is, profitability. There is no such incentive in the public sector. In fact, there is a disincentive. (Bailey, 1987, p. 150)

Two dynamics are operational here.

> In the first place, the evidence shows that public enterprises at state and local levels tend to underinvest in functionally specific plant and equipment. This propensity is reflected in low productivity growth, a characteristic of activities carried out by state and local governments, as well as in a tendency to overstaff. (Thompson, 1989, p. 205)

In addition, there is a pronounced tendency to underuse government assets (Bailey, 1987). Explanations for these forces are grounded on the following foundations. To begin with, as Hirsch (1991) demonstrates, the absence of competition and the "more rigid hierarchical structure[s]" (p. 80) that define the public sector, in and of themselves, "reduce the potential for technological improvements over the long term" (p. 80). Second, public agencies often confront severe restraints on raising capital, restrictions that are rooted in the democratic political process (Hirsch, 1991). Third, because the "capital budgetary process in most jurisdictions is separate from the operating budget process" (Bailey, 1987, p. 150), "it is more difficult to make coordinated investments in labor-saving equipment [because] the opportunities to make tradeoffs between the two is limited" (Savas, 1987, p. 112).

Pirie (1988) asserts that because "there is considerable political pressure to squeeze capital spending in order to expand current spending, political pressure tends to deny public operations the degree of capitalization which they require" (p. 24). In discussing this fourth cause of the undercapitalization of the public sector, he reveals how this phenomenon produces a government sector that "is denied new, labour-saving and cost-cutting technology" (p. 24) and is often required to make do with "outdated equipment in poor repair" (p. 30).

Finally, Darr (1991) believes that capital productivity is less viable in the public domain because private firms do a more successful job than public agencies in "purchasing more effective equipment better suited to performing specific tasks" (p. 64). He quotes Harney in his claim that "public agencies 'purchase equipment to match the budget' while private firms buy equipment 'to match the task' " (p. 64). For all these reasons, proponents of privatization maintain, governments face significant constraints that lead to the "use of less capital-intensive production technologies than they otherwise would. Consequently, they produce less efficiently in the long run" (Hirsch, 1991, p. 79).

### Quality

> The issue of whether contracting out will diminish the quality of service the public receives is of paramount importance. (Dudek & Company, 1989, p. 11)

> Government ownership and regulation result in output that is smaller and less responsive to individual wants. Thus a careful program of privatization would result in higher output and increased welfare. (De Alessi, 1987, p. 35)

> Another argument against privatization is that the quality of social services may deteriorate as private entrepreneurs seek to lower costs and increase profits. (Gormley, 1991b, p. 309)

The case is often made—and just as often challenged—that privatization will enhance the quality of the goods and services that taxpayers receive. An analysis of the expected benefits and the possible costs of privatization in the area of product and service quality is sketched out below. Once again, our intent is not to construct an empirical scoreboard but rather to provide the conceptual raw material needed to evaluate the possible quality consequences of privatization initiatives in education.

Before proceeding, however, it is necessary to underscore the importance of the quality dimension as it applies to privatization in education. Although quality of service delivery usually places a distant second to efficiency as a principal rationale for privatization (Van Horn, 1991), as one moves into the social services—such as education—efforts to improve quality take on much greater significance (Brown, 1991; Dudek & Company, 1989; Gormley, 1991a). Thus, in some cases, "distributional and output quality concerns mute the importance of efficiency in production" (Pack, 1991, p. 296). In addition, the saliency of the quality dimension is heightened when attacks on the effectiveness of service delivery are paramount in the case used to support privatization initiatives (Butler, 1991). As the next chapter reveals, this is exactly the situation confronting education today. Concomitantly, because "quality in public service tends to be a complex matter" (Donahue, 1989, pp. 83-84), it is difficult to measure (Committee on the Judiciary, 1986) and difficult to monitor (Gormley, 1991b)—much more so than are costs. The issue of quality assessment in education under privatization is, therefore, likely to be laden with difficulties.

*Possible Benefits*

Based on the theoretical propositions we examined earlier in this chapter, advocates of a larger role for the private sector in providing public goods and services assert that privatization will "produce better quality services for the price paid" (De Hoog, 1984, pp. 6-7). They claim that, because of the dynamics of the marketplace and because "many of the forces which contribute to substandard performance by state enterprises will cease to operate after the transfer is made" (Pirie, 1988, p. 54), "privatization properly implemented offers tremendous opportunities for . . . providing better services" (Poole, 1985, p. 43). At the heart of the logic here is the proposition that, "because of the sensitivity of the private sector to its customers, as opposed to the insensitivity of many publicly held operations to their customers, the private sector can [ensure] more dependable services than can public ownership" (Butler, 1991, p. 19). Privatization "ensures production of services that are demanded by consumers, not those chosen by government bureaucrats" (Smith, 1987, p. 183). Quality is thus supposedly enhanced by "more responsive service" (Savas, 1987, p. 98)—a responsiveness fostered through innovation, the development of an array of service options, and more direct attention to the needs of customers (Goldring & Sullivan, 1995; Kolderie & Hauer, 1991; Ross, 1988).

The effectiveness of service provision is also expected to improve because of "the superior flexibility . . . of privatization" (Fixler & Poole, 1987, p. 177). According to this line of analysis, because "the public sector is notoriously noninnovative and inflexible" (Pirie, 1985, p. 53), government "is slower to adopt new ideas, more hidebound in its accustomed ways, and less adaptable to changing circumstances" (Pirie, 1988, p. 28). As a consequence, quality, as measured in terms of output and customer satisfaction, leaves a good deal to be desired. Privatization would therefore heighten quality by taking advantage of the flexibility associated with markets. Particular aspects of such flexibility that are often cited include the ability to off-load costly in-house functions (Butler, 1991)—"persons with specialized skills can be obtained as needed, and without the constraints imposed by salary limitations or civil service restrictions" (Peters, 1991, p. 58); "adjust the size of a program up or down in response to changing demand and changing availability of funds" (Savas, 1987, p. 109); "purchase new equipment more quickly" (Brown, 1991, p. 273); undertake new projects more easily (Peters, 1991); and "hire, promote, reward, and even out workload peaks" (Brown, 1991, p. 273).

*A Contested Claim*

The belief that privatization and enhanced quality are tightly linked is not universally held, however. Indeed, "the contention that employing private contractors diminishes service quality" (Moore, 1987, p. 67) is frequently heard. Whereas advocates of privatization acknowledge "the potential problem of reduced quality of service" (Fixler & Poole, 1987, p. 173), opponents talk in more strident terms, arguing that the "high financial stakes [of competition] bring with them a temptation to maximize profitability by skimping on quality" (Brown, 1991, p. 274), that low cost also "buys lower quality and higher risks" (Thayer, 1987, p. 167), and that "the profit motive leads to cost-cutting practices that reduce the quality of the service" (Peters, 1991, p. 58). These critics rarely see privatization harnessed to the goal of "improve[d] public service quality" (Martin, 1993, p. 173). Where others perceive vistas of higher productivity and greater effectiveness, analysts in this camp are more likely to discern a much darker horizon—one colored by "the substitution of lower-quality resources and deliberate malfeasance" (Clarkson, 1989, p. 177). Some of these critics maintain that, at least in some cases,

> privatization may be a maneuver by city officials seeking to substitute a cheaper package of services for the fuller package that had previously been provided by civil servants. Contracting out may offer insulation against political pressures and may thus serve as a stratagem to achieve otherwise unfeasible austerity measures. (Donahue, 1989, p. 136)

Whether grounded in caution or anchored in critique, a number of specific arguments challenge the proposition that privatization will result in the production of higher quality goods and the delivery of higher quality services. Some analysts assert that, contrary to the claims of privatization advocates, "competitive environments . . . and competitive markets bring out the worst, not the best, in human behavior" (Thayer, 1987, p. 148)—that profits and quality may be in competition, and that quality will be the casualty in the long run. They fear that corners will be cut and service quality will deteriorate (President's Commission on Privatization, 1988). Others propose that privatization may lead to reduced services for certain types of consumers, especially poor ones and "clients who may be particularly difficult and expensive to help, such as disadvantaged clients" (Hatry, 1991, p. 265). Under this dynamic, known as creaming (Walters, 1987), it is believed that privatization "will result in services going only to the easy and profitable customers, while the difficult and unprofitable customers are neglected" (Kolderie, 1991, p. 255):

> Profit-seeking entrepreneurs will move in, it is claimed, "skimming off" the lucrative and profitable parts of the service, leaving those without power without a service. "Cowboys" will move in for quick money, lacking expertise and concern for safety as they scramble desperately for every penny of profit. (Pirie, 1988, p. 54)

Still others base their apprehensions about lowered quality upon conditions associated with the process of privatization. They are quick to point out the "hidden public costs associated with monitoring delivery of services" (Clarkson, 1989, p. 179) and the deterioration of process safeguards such as civil service regulations associated with the production function in the government sector (President's Commission on Privatization, 1988). In particular,

> critics of market-based programmes argue that private sector actors can more easily implement a strategy of reduced quality and levels of service than can formal governmental agencies. Although public overseeing of most public sector organizations is certainly limited, it is likely to be greater than that exercised over private service providers. (Hula, 1990b, p. 14)

These reviewers also worry that privatization strategies "may co-opt nonprofit social service agencies and cause them to downplay their role as a social conscience" (Peters, 1991, p. 59), again diminishing rather than enhancing service quality for customers.

Some analysts have also questioned the flexibility benefits often attributed to privatization, pointing out that effectiveness can be sacrificed when "contracting limits the flexibility of government in responding to emergencies" (Savas, 1987, p. 111), and when "public officials [are] locked into inflexible contracts that prevent response to unforeseen circumstances" (Darr, 1991, p. 63). Quality also can be reduced, critics argue, when reliance on the private sector leads an agency to use a variety of different contractors, thus undermining "the creation and implementation of coherent public policy" (De Hoog, 1984, p. 14).

Claims that privatization may lead to reduced, not enhanced, quality often highlight the issues of service vulnerability and accountability. The vulnerability thesis posits that privatization "fosters an undesirable dependence on contractors" (Savas, 1987, p. 111) and that these "contractors, grantees, and firms receiving franchises, are more likely to curtail, interrupt, or cease operations due to such circumstances as financial problems, strikes, and rebidding of contracts" (Brown, 1991, p. 274). It is argued that these threats to reliability (Goldring & Sullivan, 1995; Gormley, 1991a) are likely to increase as financial constraints become more pronounced (Hatry, 1991; Peters, 1991).

Although the potential of greater accountability under privatization initiatives is acknowledged (Fixler & Poole, 1987), and the more sophisticated analyses point out that both negative and positive effects in this area are possible (Hirsch, 1991), apprehension about diminished accountability remains a central strand of the privatization literature. Indeed, as Van Horn (1991) notes, "fears about the lack of accountability for service delivery are a principal impediment to new privatization ventures" (p. 277). Darr (1991) concurs, reporting that "perhaps the one issue that encompasses many of labor's concerns about privatization is that of accountability" (p. 64).

For our purposes here, the following conclusions about account-ability appear most salient. First, "there is no reason to believe that a private form of organization will always, or even usually, improve accountability" (Donahue, 1989, p. 222). Second, "in cases where society has decided that specific laws must be administered with particular care and specified outcomes must be [ensured], govern-ments in the eyes of some have regulatory advantages over private corporations" (Hirsch, 1991, p. 18): "Critics have charged that in almost any type of service it is usually more difficult for the public or program recipients to hold contractors responsible than elected officials and bureaucrats when the service proves to be unsatisfac-tory" (De Hoog, 1984, p. 14). Third, problems with accountability and control under privatization mirror accountability concerns with public sector provision—except for the fact that, under privatization, the interests of consumers and taxpayers may be relegated to the interests of corporate managers and owners rather than to those of bureaucrats and public employees. In short, "diffused accountability invites agents, however organized, to exploit the public" (Donahue, 1989, p. 92). Finally, ensuring accountability for quality through contracts can be a difficult business, especially when quality stan-dards and criteria are difficult to specify (Hirsch, 1991).

### Employees

Almost all of the literature identifies the employment issue as one of the most controversial aspects of contracting out services. (Dudek & Company, 1989, p. 15)

A report issued in June by the World Bank lent support to the view that public workers have little to fear from privatiz-ation. (Worsnop, 1992, p. 984)

Savings in real resources are generally viewed as economically beneficial to consumers because the resources released by greater efficiency can be utilized to produce more of other goods and services that consumers desire. However, some forms of productivity gains may involve exploiting or underpaying workers or other inputs in the production process, rather than improving management. In that case, output per worker may be high due to changes (in work rules, for example) that result in paying workers less than a competitive return on their investments in job specific expertise and training. (Hilke, 1992, p. 118)

*The Framework*

As Pirie (1988) succinctly concludes, "the issue of jobs is a very sensitive one" (p. 62) under privatization. It is also, as are many of the issues involved in privatization, long on opinion, short on analysis, and largely uninformed by reference to objective empirical data. However, Dudek & Company (1989) provide a useful framework for examining labor effects of privatization via contracting out, commencing from the proposition that "the contracting out option is clearly the form of privatization with the most direct and controversial impact on employment" (p. 8). The categories we employ in the remainder of this section are drawn primarily from their framework.

*Job Displacement.* The subject of job displacement is "probably the most controversial issue associated with the policy of contracting out government services" (Dudek & Company, 1989, p. 47). The crux of the issue is, What becomes of public employees when their jobs are transferred to private contractors? Philosophically speaking, advocates of privatization, while acknowledging that contracting out is unlikely to slow the public expenditure express train significantly, believe that shifting work to the private sector will garner some cost savings and efficiencies. Pragmatically, they recognize that the issue of jobs can become a "formidable obstacle for jurisdictions attempting to privatize services" (p. 47). Opponents, on the other hand, assert that contracting out will lead to widespread unemployment and an expanding emphasis on part-time work (Martin, 1993; Worsnop, 1992), as well as fewer "protective workrules" (Gomez-Ibanez et al., 1990, p. 169).

The evidence to date suggests that a variety of forces are operating to reduce job displacement associated with contracting out: (a) opposition from public employees (Clarkson, 1989; Donahue, 1989); (b) the strength of public sector unions (Donahue, 1989); (c) the willingness of public sector employees to go to the mat on the issue —to "engage in job actions or bring costly legal challenges against contracting" (Peters, 1991, p. 59); and (d) the acknowledgment by government officials of the volatility of the issue. Most states and municipalities, therefore, engage a variety of safeguards to ensure that attrition becomes the primary vehicle for reducing the public payroll under contracting (Dudek & Company, 1989; Fixler & Poole, 1991; Roehm et al., 1991), including requiring the contractor "to give current government employees the right of first refusal for most or all jobs under the contract" (Fixler & Poole, 1991, p. 82), focusing contracts on new and expanding services (Dudek & Company, 1989), and requiring any displaced workers to be absorbed by other municipal agencies. As a result, "on average only about 5 percent to 10 percent of public employees affected by government contracting are laid off [because of] this alternative delivery approach" (Dudek & Company, 1989, p. 2).

However, there is no reason to assume that the past will be prologue to the future in matters of job displacement. If the conditions supporting the creation of safeguards deteriorate, so might the safeguards themselves. Furthermore, there is little evidence about the long-term effects of worker displacement (Dudek & Company, 1989). Although it is possible that initially unemployed workers later secure gainful employment, it is also possible that initially relocated employees may be dismissed later by their new employers.

*Wages and Benefits.* While drawing attention to variation among government agencies, Dudek & Company (1989) conclude that "private contractors generally pay lower wages than do the government agencies they replace" (p. 2). Reports tracking salaries in industries undergoing privatization via deregulation (e.g., the trucking and airline industries) uncover similar declines in wages (Thayer, 1987). Initial analyses of the effects of privatization on fringe benefits are even more pronounced: Because "the government usually provides much more generous fringe benefits than do contractors . . . the largest difference between the government and the contractor is in the level of the fringe benefits provided" (Dudek & Company, 1989, p. 3). In one of the most thoughtful discussions of this issue, Donahue (1989) demonstrates that, for most services, especially labor-intensive ones such as education, "lower labor costs—both wages and benefits—are a major part of the contractor cost edge" (p. 144).

*Minority Impact.* Because "governments tend to be more aggressive than private contractors about hiring and promoting minorities and women" (Martin, 1993, p. 179), some analysts are concerned that "any negative effects of contracting out [will] fall with particular force on women and minorities who are employed in great numbers by public agencies and [who] often earn better pay than they could in the private sector" (Worsnop, 1992, p. 982), and "that privatization will cause proportionately more job losses and fewer opportunities for minority workers" (Savas, 1987, p. 102) (see also Martin, 1993). Analysis on this point is limited, with some reviewers claiming that "the job opportunities for members of minorities appear to be pretty similar regardless of the arrangement" (Savas, 1987, p. 104) and others concluding that "contracting out might impede black professional employment opportunities" (Dudek & Company, 1989, p. 29).

*Professionalism.* The issue of privatization's effects on professionalism in the workforce has not received much attention to date. Ismael (1988) maintains that "one impact of contracting out of public services to the private sector has been identified as the deprofessionalization of the public sector" (p. 7), and others raise this possibility as well (Committee on the Judiciary, 1986; Florestano, 1991). Yet we have almost no data to test this hypothesis—a hypothesis with special significance for public sector fields like education that are more professional than bureaucratic.

Donahue (1989) summarizes our knowledge of the connection between privatization and public employees:

> Two facts are equally evident: Delegating certain functions to private firms usually saves tax dollars, and much of these savings [come] at the expense of public employees. . . . In short, a good deal of what taxpayers stand to gain from privatization comes at the expense of municipal employees. (p. 145)

*Interpretation*

One of the most distinct features of all these analyses is their subjectivity; that is, how one views the effects of privatization on labor has a good deal to do with the mindset that one brings to the problem. Those who see public employees as hardworking, dedicated civil servants tend to view privatization with considerable alarm. They believe that "commercialization has been employed mainly as a weapon against public sector workers" (Martin, 1993, p. 173):

> Public sector workers the world over have seen their jobs, pay and service conditions under constant siege. . . . What has tended to happen . . . is that instead of encouraging and helping public service workers to do a better and more satisfying job, the new managerialism has attacked them. Instead of providing them with tools, "business practices" have fashioned weapons against them. (p. 14)

Likewise, those on the inside looking out (i.e., public employees) are extremely skeptical of privatization initiatives such as contracting out. They "fear losing control of their agency's performance, not to mention their own jobs" (Pack, 1991, p. 297).

> Defenders of public employee unionization charge that this method of service delivery is a way of by-passing the municipal and state unions to use underpaid, nonunion labor. When governments decide to switch from public employees to private firms, union leaders accuse the offending agency of union-busting and putting public employees on welfare. (De Hoog, 1984, p. 14)

"Public employees overwhelmingly look upon privatization with suspicion or hostility. Their attitude flows from the belief that the contracting out of services or sale of government assets brings lower wages and fringe benefits and fewer opportunities for advancement" (Worsnop, 1992, p. 982). Both defenders of public employees and those employees themselves assert that "contracting nullifies the basic principle of merit employment and subverts laws regarding veterans['] preference in government employment; it is demoralizing to employees, deprives government of the skills it needs in-house, and therefore is fundamentally debilitating of government capability" (Savas, 1987, p. 110). They see privatization as "a modern and sophisticated version of what was once called 'scabbing' and associated with 'strike-breaking' and 'union-busting' " (Thayer, 1987, p. 168).

Reviewers examining the information with different frames of reference arrive at quite different conclusions. Those who maintain that employees possess an unfair "advantage in the public sector in terms of job security, working conditions and fringe benefits" (Pirie, 1988, p. 59)—who believe that workers "are much better off in the public sector [and] know it" (Worsnop, 1992, p. 982)—discern gains from privatization where defenders of the public sector see costs. This group includes a variety of perspectives. Some believe that public agencies enjoy "monopoly rents allowed by regulation . . . in the form of higher salaries, reduced hours, and attractive fringe benefits" (Smith, 1987, p. 186). Others focus on restrictive civil service regulations and unchecked and hard-to-control collective bargaining in the public sector that they believe gives unfair advantage to public employees (Bailey, 1991; Ramsey, 1987; Savas, 1987). Still others question the income redistribution dimensions of public employment (Donahue, 1989; Worsnop, 1992) that may enhance the position of government workers vis-à-vis their private sector colleagues. Finally, some are troubled by the "political pressure" (Ramsey, 1987, p. 95) that they believe public employees use to distort the budget portfolio in favor of labor and at the expense of capital investments and technological innovations (Hirsch, 1991; Ramsey, 1987). For all these reasons, analysts in this group underscore the benefits of "disarm[ing] public trade unions that are abusing a monopoly position" (Hemming & Mansoor, 1988, p. 6) and "put[ting] personnel practices outside the civil service system and public collective bargaining" (Bailey, 1987, p. 146).

## Values

The preeminent question in the debate over privatization concerns the values that privatization promotes. (Starr, 1991, p. 27)

All markets are not the same, and where public institutions
have assumed important democratic functions, the shift toward market alternatives may jeopardize core values of our
society. (President's Commission on Privatization, 1988, p. 22)

Sometimes lurking in the background and at other times at the
forefront of the picture, questions of values are central to the debate
on privatization. Although these value issues are often treated in a
less sophisticated manner than are other topics examined in this
chapter, such as efficiency and quality, and are less informed by data
from actual privatization initiatives, it would be inappropriate to
complete our analysis without touching on the most central of these
values: choice, equity, and community.

Before beginning, however, it is important to note that the value
debate in the privatization literature is heavily skewed in favor of
public provision. This is the case for at least three reasons. First, value
issues are generally of greater importance to proponents of government. Thus, critics of privatization are much more likely to write
about values, whereas advocates tend to focus on other criteria,
especially efficiency and quality. Second, value discussions nearly
always begin with certain givens (e.g., opportunity for equal participation, the importance of the public good) that are, in fact, essential
building blocks of government service. Third, those who analyze
value questions regularly enlarge their discussions to include the
social goals and objectives that often become important aspects of
government service (e.g., employment of underrepresented groups).
For all these reasons, debates on values, with the exception of choice,
rarely occur on a level playing field.

*Choice*

The case for privatization includes other claims besides improved efficiency, budget savings, and increased economic
growth. The key word is *choice*. (Starr, 1987, p. 131)

As Gormley (1991b) has observed, "Choice is a popular value for
both proponents and opponents of privatization" (p. 309). On one
side, advocates assert that "a large public sector . . . necessarily reduces the scope of total freedom by limiting economic freedom and

by reducing the effectiveness of the countervailing force of the market on potentially tyrannical political power" (Berry & Lowery, 1987, p. 5). Proponents believe "that privatization will enlarge the range of choice for individuals while serving the same essential functions as do traditional programs" (Starr, 1987, p. 131). By "maximiz[ing] individual preferences" (Hula, 1990b, p. 7), they assert, "choice offers the prospect of greater satisfaction with services freely chosen by those who will receive them" (Gormley, 1991a, p. 8). Even critics acknowledge the benefits of choice, recognizing that the severe restrictions imposed by uniform public programs—welfare loss resulting from collective consumption in economic terms—makes choice "unquestionably the single strongest point in the case for privatization" (Starr, 1987, p. 131).

At the same time, however, "the supposed freedom advantages of limited government has also attracted critical comment" (Berry & Lowery, 1987, p. 7); that is, the potential costs of privatization in this area have not gone uncataloged. Those who are most effective in challenging the expected benefits of choice do not tackle the issue head on. Rather, they switch playing fields completely—from markets to the polity and then replay the game. According to Starr (1991), for example, "the market and polity represent two different moral frameworks for choice" (p. 27). He argues that "privatization does not transform constraint into choice; it transfers decisions from one realm of choice and constraint to another" (1987, p. 132), a switch that most advocates of privatization herald and most critics decry. By examining choice from the moral framework of the polity, Starr (1987) concludes that

> privatization diminishes the sphere of public information, deliberation, and accountability—elements of democracy whose value is not reducible to efficiency. If we are to respect preferences, as conservatives urge that we do, we ought to respect preferences for democratic over market choice where they have been long and consistently demonstrated. (p. 132)

Critics also maintain that because of the need for considerable regulation in sensitive social services (Gormley, 1991b) and because of "private loss-leading" (Bell & Cloke, 1990, p. 12) tactics, market-based choice may be more illusionary than advocates suggest.

*Equity*

> Issues of distributional fairness (or equity) are commonly invoked as criteria of program effectiveness. (Ross, 1988, p. 12)

> Proponents of privatization maintain that greater choice would serve the interests of equity. (Starr, 1987, p. 131)

"The effects of the privatization decision on equity" (Hirsch, 1991, p. 69) are the subject of some debate and confusion—confusion increased by the fact that "equity can be interpreted and measured in many reasonable ways" (Ross, 1988, p. 15). The positive case for linkage between privatization and equity, defined here as a fair "distribution of society's material resources" (p. 14), usually takes one of two forms. On the weaker end of the continuum, advocates simply argue that the current equity landscape remains largely unchanged when production is shifted from public agencies to private firms (Dudek & Company, 1989). More aggressively, they assert that because the rich currently enjoy privileges (such as better schools and better health care) not available to others, "greater freedom of choice will generally lead to a more just distribution of benefits" (Starr, 1987, p. 131). They also suggest that because minority groups

> are more dependent on government-provided services than wealthier groups, and they rely more on private goods that have been collectivized, to the extent the minority groups on average have lower median incomes any arrangement that results in better quality of service, or in more cost-effective service (which makes more money available to government) is likely to benefit minority groups more. (Savas, 1987, p. 104)

Critics of privatization, not surprisingly, are less sanguine about the impact of privatization on the distribution of society's resources. They feel that "when distributive justice is at issue, privatization signals a diminished commitment to include the poor in the national household" (Starr, 1987, p. 135). Rather than advancing the equity agenda, these analysts are concerned that "a large-scale shift of public services to private providers would contribute to further isolating the least advantaged" (p. 134), leaving them with a poorer public sector providing services of a last resort (Starr, 1987, 1991). In addition, they remind us that "concern with distributional implications of denying disadvantaged groups opportunities for public employment [can]not [be] readily dismissed" (Hirsch, 1991, p. 138), and that privatization initiatives such as "contracting will result in disproportionate job losses among members of minority communities, many of whom are government employees" (Savas, 1987, p. 111). At the heart of this apprehension is the fear that "distributional social goals" (Pack, 1991, p. 304) that are a key aspect of many public services may be jettisoned when activities are privatized (Pack, 1991; Ross, 1988).

## Community

When people actually begin to see the benefits of privatization in practice, they may glimpse . . . strategies and tools with which to harness the private sector for public good. (Fitzgerald, 1988, p. 22)

The priorities and ethos of public service are being commercialized. (Martin, 1993, p. 1)

Although some analysts believe that "it is difficult to regard privatization as a threat to democratic government" (Gormley, 1991b, p. 317), critics of privatization foresee unpleasant effects on community and democracy as privatization initiatives take root: Privatization proposals are "attacked as further eroding the sense of community in contemporary society and for intensifying the individualistic ethic of our time" (Kolderie, 1991, p. 257). Of particular concern is the fear that through "the removal of decisions from the public arena" (Starr, 1987, p. 132) and "by substituting private preferences for collective choices" (Gormley, 1991b, p. 317), privatization could "diminish the individual incentive for participation" (Starr, 1987, p. 132) and thus "drain much of the energy and life from local government" (President's Commission on Privatization, 1988, p. 22), "rob us of the advantages of public deliberation and discussion" (Gormley, 1991b, p. 317), and "weaken the foundations of local democracy" (Starr, 1987, p. 133). According to Bailey (1987), the result will be that "a sense of public legitimacy will have been squandered for marginal productivity enhancement—a trade-off that not only is unquantifiable but is even more dangerous to effective governance" (p. 151).

> Traditionally, the political world has offered a way to engage with others that is different from private life, a form of engagement known as democracy. The sense of empowerment that we gain whenever we become participants in the creation of our social and political world will be lost if we withdraw even further into our private lives or commercial dealings. (Frug, 1991, p. 308)

> This is one of the things that ought to concern us about privatization: the desiccated vision of democratic politics that the privatization movement implicitly promotes. (Starr, 1991, p. 28)

For all these reasons, critics of privatization believe that "democratic political choice offers better prospects for civic discovery" (Gormley, 1991a, p. 12) than do appeals to markets.

## Conclusion

This chapter was devoted to two central tasks. Initially, drawing heavily upon the public choice literature, we examined the theoretical underpinnings of the privatization movement. We reviewed in some detail both the economic and political foundations of public choice theory, especially market theory and the political dimensions of bureaucracy and representative governance. In the second half of the chapter, we investigated at a conceptual level the potential benefits and costs of privatization in four broad areas: efficiency, quality, effects on employees, and values. We turn our attention in the final chapter to a review of the specific forces supporting privatization initiatives in education.

# FORCES FUELING
# PRIVATIZATION IN
# EDUCATION

# 6

Existing structures for schooling cannot produce the kind of changes necessary to make a substantial difference. (Mojkowski & Fleming, 1988, p. 1)

The first chapters of this volume investigated the topic of privatization in a comprehensive and general manner. For the most part, what was discussed there could apply equally well to firefighting and waste disposal. This final chapter of the book[1] turns the analytic spotlight directly on the privatization of education and specifically the forces that are fueling the privatization movement in education.

Calls for market-based solutions to the reform of education emanate from a variety of quarters. Those demands, in turn, draw strength from conditions that define the environment of schooling and from the efforts of an assortment of stakeholders to radically overhaul the existing educational system. In this chapter, we study these forces in some detail. We begin our analysis with perhaps the most critical issue—the failing health of education and pleas for improvement. We then examine three trends dominating the environment in which schools are embedded—the perceived crisis in the economy, the changing social fabric of the nation, and the evolution to postindustrial perspectives on politics and organizations—that have created a particularly hospitable climate for privatization initiatives. In the final section, we chronicle how the struggle to reinvent schooling is also encouraging the consideration of reform strategies that strike at the heart of schooling as a public monopoly.

## The Failing Health of Schooling

Public education consumes nearly 7% of our gross national product. Its expenditures have doubled or tripled in every postwar decade, even when enrollments declined. I can't think of any other single sector of American society that has absorbed more money by serving fewer people with steadily declining service. (Kearnes, 1988b, p. 566)

Supporting nearly all the privatization proposals are strident critiques of the overall effectiveness of the educational system, as well as of the particular dimensions and elements of schooling that have contributed to this failure. Reformers have generally used seven outcome measures to document unsatisfactory school effectiveness: (a) academic achievement in basic subject areas compared to historical data about the United States and to student performance in other countries; (b) functional literacy; (c) preparation for employment; (d) the holding power of schools (dropout rates); (e) knowledge of specific subject areas such as geography and economics; (f) mastery of higher order skills; and (g) initiative, responsibility, and citizenship (Murphy, 1990). Indexes in each of these performance dimensions are contained in Table 6.1. Collectively, the data provide a not-very-reassuring portrait of the health of the American educational system.

From our perspective here, the important issue is that some reformers contend that these results are linked to a series of causes —the depersonalization of schooling, hierarchical management systems, a moribund production function, and an absence of accountability—that can be traced to the public monopoly status of education and that can be addressed by market-based reform initiatives. It is this belief in the efficacy of market-based solutions that is

(text continues on page 149)

**TABLE 6.1** Indexes of School Failure

| Area | Source |
|---|---|
| *Student Achievement* (historical and cross-national comparisons) | |
| "The National Assessment of Educational Progress (NAEP) revealed a dismal record for 17-year-olds between 1971 and 1982. Test scores reported by the NAEP showed steady declines in vocabulary, reading, and mathematics." | Association for Supervision and Curriculum Development (1986, p. 19) |
| "International comparisons of student achievement, completed a decade ago, reveal that on 19 academic tests American students were never first or second and were last seven times." | National Commission on Excellence in Education (1983, p. 8) |
| "U.S. eighth graders' math skills rank ninth among twelve major industrialized countries of the world." | National Governors' Association (1986, p. 5) |
| "United States 13-year-olds finished last in a six nation study of math and science skills." | *USA Today* (1 February 1989, p. 1) |
| "Average achievement of high school students on most standardized tests is now lower than 26 years ago when Sputnik was launched." | National Commission on Excellence in Education (1983, p. 8) |
| "America's top high school science students ranked below those of nearly all other countries in a new comparison of scores from an international test released here last week." | *Education Week* (19 March 1988, p. 4) |
| "American 12th graders studying biology scored below students from the 16 other countries included in the analysis, which examined data from a 24-nation science assessment administered in 1986." | |
| "In chemistry, the study found students from all other countries except Canada and Finland out-scored their U.S. counterparts." | |

*(continued)*

**Table 6.1** Continued

| Area | Source |
|------|--------|
| "And in physics, only those two countries and Sweden ranked below the United States." | |
| "The achievement levels are particularly 'discouraging,' the study's authors note, since the American students in the comparison were drawn from the small proportion of the nation's high-school students enrolled in advanced science courses." | |
| "At a time when economic growth is increasingly dependent on mastery of science and technology, U.S. eighth graders' knowledge and understanding of mathematics is below that of most of their counterparts in other industrialized countries (12 out of 14)." | Carnegie Forum on Education and the Economy (1986, p. 16) |
| "Despite achievement gains over the past decade, particularly among minority students, American high-school students display a 'dismal' level of mathematics proficiency, the National Assessment of Educational Progress reported last week." | *Education Week* (15 June 1988, p. 1) |
| "About half of all 17-year-olds tested in 1986 were unable to perform 'moderately complex' procedures usually taught in junior high school, such as finding averages and interpreting graphs, the assessment found. Only 6 percent were able to solve multi-step problems." | |
| "In addition, NAEP's report says, an 'alarming' number of 13-year-olds lack the skills in whole-number computation needed for everyday tasks, and approximately 7,000,000 of the 3rd and 4th graders who took the test 'have not yet acquired an understanding of rudimentary mathematical skills and concepts.'" | |
| "These results, which federal officials last week called 'tragic' and 'sobering,' are consistent with those of a 1982 international mathematics assessment, which found that U.S. students lagged far behind those of other industrialized nations." | |
| "The data suggest, according to the report, that students'—and the nation's—economic future may be in jeopardy." | |

"Moreover, contrary to widespread opinion, it isn't clear that our top students compare well with the top students of other nations. As Magnet (1988, p. 86) notes, 'the top 5% of the U.S. 12th-graders who took international calculus and algebra tests in 1982 came in dead last among the top 12th-graders of nine developed countries.'"

Boyd & Hartman (1987)

### Basic Literacy

"It is not unusual for one-third of college freshman in the U.S. to read below a seventh grade level."

National Governors' Association (1986, p. 5)

"As we move into another Presidential election year, it's sobering to note that America's public schools graduate 700,000 functionally illiterate kids every year—and that 700,000 more drop out. Four out of five young adults in a recent survey couldn't summarize the main point of a newspaper article, read a bus schedule, or figure their change from a restaurant bill."

Kearnes (1988a, p. 566)

"The NAEP reading assessment . . . measured progress at three achievement levels: advanced, proficient, and basic. . . . only 25, 28 and 37 percent of America's students in grades 4, 8, and 12, respectively met or exceeded the proficient level for reading."

Network News and Views (November, 1991, p. iii)

"More than two-thirds of the nation's 4th-, 8th-, and 12th-grade students—including one-quarter of high school seniors—are not proficient readers, according to the latest results from the National Assessment of Educational Progress."

Education Week (22 September 1992, p. 1)

"It found that, nationwide, more than a quarter of the 4th graders failed to demonstrate the ability to perform simple arithmetic reasoning with whole numbers."

Education Week (12 June 1991, p. 1)

"Results from the recent National Adult Literacy Survey suggest that 47 percent of America's adult population possesses low literacy levels."

Network News and Views (November 1993, p. i)

### Preparation for Employment

"The business community blamed the schools for failing to prepare students adequately in basic skills. In fact, business leaders charged that the decline in achievement paralleled the decline in performance of American workers."

Association for Supervision and Curriculum Development (1986, p. 20)

(continued)

**Table 6.1** Continued

| Area | Source |
| --- | --- |
| "I believe the success of that second wave of reform is critical, because public education has put this country at a terrible competitive disadvantage. The American workforce is running out of qualified people. If current demographic and economic trends continue, American business will have to hire a million new workers a year who can't read, write, or count. Teaching them how—and absorbing the lost productivity while they're learning—will cost industry $25 billion a year for as long as it takes. And nobody I know can say how long that will be. Teaching new workers basic skills is doing the schools' product-recall work for them. And frankly, I resent it." | Kearnes (1988a, p. 566) |
| "While American business has no place telling educators how to run schools, we have two very legitimate roles: The first is to say that the output of your schools is not good enough to do the work we need done." | Gerstner, cited in *Education Week* (18 May 1994, p. 6) |
| "Up to 40 percent of the nation's manufacturing firms say their efforts to upgrade workplace technology and increase productivity have been stymied by the low level of education of their workforce, according to a new study by the National Association of Manufacturers.<br><br>Because of employee-skill deficiency, the survey indicates, 40 percent of firms are having serious problems upgrading technology, 37 percent are having difficulty raising productivity, and 30 percent have not been able to reorganize into a high-performance workplace by giving employees more responsibility.<br><br>Businesses also said they reject five out of six job candidates and have found shortages of skilled and semiskilled workers throughout the country, with shortages expected to become severe by 1996." | *Education Week* (11 December, 1991, p. 5) |
| "The study, based on Carnegie's first international survey of higher-education faculties, found only about 20 percent of U.S. professors agreeing with the statement, 'Undergraduates are adequately prepared in written- and oral-communication skills.' Just 15 percent of U.S. faculty members agreed with a similar statement about mathematics and quantitative reasoning." | *Education Week* (22 June 1993, p. 12) |

"As a major contributor of tax dollars to public education, corporate America is getting a lousy return on its investment. Not only are schools today not preparing kids for jobs, they aren't even teaching them to read and write."

Perry (1988, p. 38)

"In the U.S., 30% of all high school students—one million teenagers each year—drop out before graduating. Most are virtually unemployable. Of those who do graduate, many do not have the problem-solving skills to function in an increasingly complex information society."

"Unfortunately, the vast majority of the schools are about the same as they were 10 years ago. The return on investment in education is minimal when one applies real quality-control measurements to the public school system."

Bowsher, cited in *Education Week* (13 October 1993, p. 8)

"More than half of small businesses have problems finding applicants for entry-level positions who possess the basic skills needed for the jobs, according to a survey by the National Alliance of Business.

*Education Week* (20 May 1992, p. 2)

The survey of 233 companies with 500 or fewer employees found that 70 percent reported difficulty finding applicants with sufficient writing skills to handle an entry-level job.

About 62 percent of those responding had trouble finding applicants with the necessary math skills, and 59 percent reported problems finding potential employees with sufficient reading skills."

"The USA's most powerful business leaders today tackle a crisis that threatens everyone's future: a near-total breakdown in our public schools."

*USA Today* (3 February 1989, p. 1B)

"'We simply don't have any more time to wait,' says Owen 'Brad' Butler, retired chairman of Procter & Gamble Co."

"U.S. corporations spend $25 billion a year teaching employees skills they should have learned at school. Motorola spends $50 million a year teaching seventh-grade math and English to 2,500 factory workers—half its hourly employees. Kodak is teaching 2,500 how to read and write."

*(continued)*

**Table 6.1** Continued

| Area | Source |
|---|---|
| *Holding Power* | |
| "Large numbers of American children are in limbo—ignorant of the past and unprepared for the future. Many are dropping out—not just out of school but out of productive society." | Carnegie Forum on Education and the Economy (1986, p. 2) |
| "Large numbers of drop-outs have become a serious problem." | |
| "In the U.S., 30% of all high school students—one million teenagers each year—drop out before graduating." | |
| "The percentage of Hispanics ages 25 and older who have completed high school . . . remains just 51 percent." | |
| *Knowledge of Specific Subject Areas* | |
| *Geography:* "A 1987 survey of 5,000 high school seniors in eight major cities produced equally dismal results. In Boston, 39% of the students couldn't name the six New England states; in Minneapolis-St. Paul, 63% couldn't name all seven continents; in Dallas, 25% couldn't identify the country that borders the U.S. to the south." | Kearnes (1988a, p. 566) |
| *Economics:* "A new survey by the Gallup Organization has found high rates of 'economic illiteracy' among 12th-grade students, college seniors, and the general public.<br>  According to the results of the poll, which were released last week by a national economics education group, the general population could correctly answer only 39 percent, and high school seniors only 35 percent, of 19 multiple-choice and open-ended questions about fundamental economics issues." | |
| *History:* "Results of the history test were, in Mr. Finn's words, 'accurate but reprehensible.' Overall, public-school students answered 54 percent of all questions correctly, with college-bound public-school students answering 60 percent correctly." | *Education Week* (9 March, 1988, p. 7) |

"For nonpublic schools, the results were only slightly better, he said, with an overall average of 60 percent and an average for independent-school students of 63 percent."

*Literature:* "On the literature assessment, public-school students answered an average of 51 percent of the questions correctly, with college-bound public-school students averaging 57 percent. The average score for students in nonpublic schools was 58 percent, and for those in independent schools 60 percent."

"'I consider a score in the low 60's on this a D minus,' Mr. Finn said."

Education Testing Service (1994, p. 1)

*Writing:* Most American students have trouble getting their ideas across in writing, according to a new National Assessment of Educational Progress report.

The results from the *NAEP 1992 Writing Report Card* show that even the best students who are able to write informative and narrative pieces have trouble preparing arguments and evidence in persuasive writing tasks. In general, fewer than 20 percent of the students wrote "elaborated" (well-developed and detailed) responses.

*Science:* "There was a steady decline in science achievement scores of U.S. 17-year-olds as measured by national assessments of science in 1969, 1973, and 1977."

National Commission on Excellence in Education (1983, p. 9)

*Science:* "Only about 1 in 20 American adults is 'scientifically literate' and can answer such basic questions as whether the earth revolves around the sun, whether antibiotics kill viruses, and whether astrology is scientific, a federally funded study has found."

"The findings, released here last week at the annual meeting of the American Association for the Advancement of Science, are similar to those of two previous U.S. studies, in 1979 and 1985."

*Education Week* (25 January 1989, p. 25)

*Science and Mathematics:* "American 13-year-olds performed at or near the bottom on a new six-nation international mathematics and science assessment, according to a federally funded study released here last week."

"Their performance on the math assessment was the poorest recorded, and on the science assessment narrowly surpassed only that of test takers from Ireland and the French-speaking portions of Ontario and New Brunswick."

*Education Week* (8 February, 1989, p. 5)

*(continued)*

**Table 6.1** Continued

| Area | Spource |
|---|---|
| *Science:* "American students' 'distressingly low' levels of achievement in science may signal the need for fundamental changes in the way the subject is taught, according to a study released last week by the National Assessment of Educational Progress." | *Education Week* (28 September, 1989, p. 1) |
| "The study showed that, despite gains over the past four years, particularly among minorities, a majority of high-school students 'are poorly equipped for informed citizenship and productive performance in the workplace.'" | |
| "And, it said, only 7 percent have the knowledge and skills necessary to perform well in college-level science courses." | |
| "In addition, the study found that almost half of the 13-year-olds tested lacked a grasp of the basic elements of science, and that nearly 30 percent of the 9-year-olds—representing 1 million students—'have not yet developed some understanding of scientific principles and a rudimentary knowledge of plants and animals.'" | |
| "'The data in this report present a situation that can only be described as a national disgrace,' said Bassam Z. Shakhashiri, director of the science- and engineering-education directorate of the National Science Foundation, at a press conference here." | |
| *Mastery of Higher Order Skills* | |
| "The Nation that dramatically and boldly led the world into the age of technology is failing to provide its own children with the intellectual tools needed for the 21st century." | National Science Board (1983, p. v) |
| "As jobs requiring little skill are automated or go offshore, and demands increase for the highly skilled, the pool of educated and skilled people grows smaller and smaller and the backwater of the unemployable rises." | Carnegie Forum on Education and the Economy (1986, p. 2) |

146

"Between 1971 and 1982, there was a net loss of 9-, 13-, and 17-year-olds' knowledge about and ability to use scientific principles. And there has been no improvement in advanced mathematical problem-solving ability."

National Governors' Association (1986, p. 5)

"Only 5 percent of the high-school seniors demonstrated the skills needed for high-technology or college-level work, officials noted."

Education Week (12 June, 1991, p. 1)

"Between one-third and two-thirds of students perform poorly on mathematics questions that require them to take time to reason and to explain their answers, a new analysis of data from the 1992 National Assessment of Educational Progress suggests."

Education Week (8 September, 1993, p. 16)

"Fewer than 20 percent of our fourth and twelfth graders understand complex mathematical problems."

Network News and Views (November 1993, p. i)

"Only 11 percent of high school seniors who took the American College Testing Program test this year are prepared for college-level calculus, and one in four will need remedial mathematics in college, a study released last week by the testing firm indicates.

Even many of those intending to pursue math and science degrees lack the necessary math background, the study found. Among seniors who said they planned to major in subjects such as engineering, computer science, and physical sciences, only a fourth earned A.C.T. scores that indicated they could enter calculus, while 14 percent would need remedial math."

"On the other hand, in the K-12 system," he [Paul E. Barton] added, "there are so few students at the top of achievement levels, and this top itself is unremarkable. And where we do have talent in the pipeline, it leaks as it flows to the higher-education system."

"Six-and-one-half percent of our 17-year-olds can solve multi-step problems and algebra," Mr. Barton said.

"That's not calculus and trigonometry."

Education Week (16 September, 1992, p. 11)

(continued)

**Table 6.1** Continued

| Area | Source |
|------|--------|
| *Initiative, Responsibility, and Citizenship* | |
| "Too many young people are leaving the schools without . . . self-discipline or purpose." | |
| "An 'unacceptably high' number of 15- to 30-year-olds are willing to lie, cheat, and steal, a new survey involving nearly 9,000 teenagers and adults nationwide suggests. | |
| The survey found that 33 percent of the high school students questioned and 16 percent of the college students said they had stolen merchandise from a store within the past year. | |
| About one-third of the students in each group said they were willing to lie on a résumé, a job application, or during a job interview to get a job they want. And 16 percent of the high school students said they had already done so at least once. | |
| Such unethical behaviors also apparently extend to school; 61 percent of the high school students and 32 percent of college students admitted having cheated on an examination once in the past year." | |
| "Student behavior and attitudes, ranging from lack of motivation to large number of drop-outs, became a serious problem." | Association for Supervision and Curriculum Development (1986, p. 9) |

moving privatization strategies closer to the forefront as a solution to the problems confronting schooling.

## A Changing Environment

A turbulent environment generates a host of highly salient demands and the system is pressed to search for solutions to a cluster of seemingly intractable problems. (Malen, Ogawa, & Kranz, 1989, p. 6)

We have truly reached a crisis moment in the social and economic history of this country. (Ramsey, interview in *Education Week*, 1992a, p. 6)

As mentioned in the previous chapters, deregulation, contracting, and voucher initiatives have appeared on the landscape as alternatives to existing political and managerial systems that define —and appear to be failing—education. Concomitantly, pressure to adopt more market-sensitive modes of operating schools draws considerable energy from movements in the larger environment surrounding education. Three of these forces have particular relevance for schools: the perceived crisis in the economy, the changing social fabric of the nation, and the movement to a postindustrial world. All three conditions lend momentum to the demand for educational reform in general (Murphy, 1990, 1991), and all three are regularly referenced by analysts of the privatization movement that is gaining a toehold in education. We treat each in turn below.

### The Perceived Crisis in the Economy

In many countries the most recent educational debate has been conducted in a context of alarm regarding the state of the economy and national competitiveness. (Chapman, 1990, p. 241)

No aspect of the environment has molded education over the past 15 years more than the economy, more specifically, the perceived deterioration of our economic well-being as a nation. There is a pervasive feeling afoot that the United States is losing, and perhaps has already lost, its foremost position in the world economy, and that its "once unchallenged preeminence in commerce, industry, science, and technological innovation" (National Commission on Excellence in Education, 1983, p. 5) has taken a terrible battering. Evidence of this belief is omnipresent in the reform documents that fueled the educational reform movement of the 1980s:

> Today, however, our faith in change—and our faith in ourselves as the world's supreme innovators—is being shaken. Japan, West Germany and other relatively new industrial powers have challenged America's position on the leading edge of change and technical invention. In the seventies, productivity in manufacturing industries grew nearly four times as fast in Japan, and twice as fast in West Germany and France, as in the United States.
>     The possibility that other nations may outstage us in inventiveness and productivity is suddenly troubling Americans. (Education Commission of the States, 1983, p. 13)

> Already the quality of our manufactured products, the viability of our trade, our leadership in research and development, and our standards of living are strongly challenged. Our children could be stragglers in a world of technology. We must not let this happen; America must not become an industrial dinosaur. (National Science Board, 1983, p. v)

> America's ability to compete in world markets is eroding. The productivity growth of our competitors outdistances our own. The capacity of our economy to provide a high standard of living is increasingly in doubt. (Carnegie Forum on Education and the Economy, 1986, p. 2)

"Whilst there has been no proven relationship between educational achievement measured by specific tests and international productivity comparisons" (Chapman, 1990, p. 241), underlying much current policy talk about privatization is "an assumption that ineffective schools are to blame for the perceived lack of competitiveness of the U.S. economy" (Tyack, 1993, p. 24).

The 1980s will be remembered for two developments: the beginning of a sweeping reassessment of the basis of the nation's economic strength and an outpouring of concern for the quality of American education. The connection between these two streams of thought is strong and growing. (Carnegie Forum on Education and the Economy, 1986, p. 11)

If only to keep and improve on the slim competitive edge we still retain in world markets, we must dedicate ourselves to the reform of our educational system. (National Commission on Excellence in Education, 1983, p. 7)

This assumption of a tight, and causal, linkage between schooling and the economy has helped produce three outcomes. First, blame has been heaped on schools. The economy is failing and schools are held responsible: The "educational systems [are] providing neither an adequate nor relevant education" (S. B. Lawton, 1991, p. 6). As reported earlier, considerable evidence has been amassed to document both sides of the equation—a deteriorating economy on one side and a failing educational system on the other.

Second, a rationale for the failure has been constructed. Analyses show that teachers and administrators are drawn from the bottom of the intellectual barrel and then poorly trained for their roles. Conditions of employment for teachers are unprofessional and stifling. The basic operating structure of schools is inadequate. The management of the enterprise has been found to be wanting, especially in providing leadership. The curriculum is a mess, lacking both rigor and coherence. Instruction is poor; materials (textbooks) worse. Students are allowed to drift through school unchallenged and uneducated. And, as bad as school is for almost everyone, it is even worse for less advantaged and minority pupils. Everywhere are intellectual softness, a lack of expectations and standards, and the absence of accountability. In short, it is not difficult to figure out why students subjected to these conditions should fare so poorly in comparison to students from other nations, their peers from other eras, and acceptable standards of performance.

Finally, and paradoxically, "in the face of [this] rising national concern for school productivity" (Guthrie, 1986, p. 305), reformers have turned their attention to the very institutions they chastise, asking them to jump-start the faltering economy:

Many reforms reflect the assumption that quality education is a key element in the development of a stable national economy, which in turn is a critical factor in our national security. American productivity has become a political issue, and education is seen as a major factor in improving productivity. (Association for Supervision and Curriculum Development, 1986, p. 2)

Whereas reformers originally placed their bets for improvement on state-developed and mandated requirements, over the past decade, more radical and more consumer-grounded strategies that "reflect the utilitarian assumptions of human capital theory" (S. B. Lawton, 1991, p. 19) have gained increasing acceptance in the reform arena. As economic problems continue to plague society, and as political and educational responses appear less effective than hoped, more radical initiatives—of which privatization is the most radical—are being weighed (Murphy, 1993a).

## Changing Social Fabric

These data have implications for educators, Ms. Weitz said, noting that, "if we're serious about education reform, we have to also deal with other risks children experience, because in the end it will affect the performance of students." (Cohen, 1992b, p. 14)

The fabric of American society is being rewoven in some places and is unraveling in others, resulting in changes that promise to have a significant impact on schooling. At the macro level, schools operate in an environment where social capital for increasing numbers of students and their families is limited:

Nearly four million American children are growing up in communities that jeopardize their safety and decrease their chances of success in school, family life, and the workplace. (Cohen, 1994, p. 5)

The economic status of America's children has declined significantly in comparison with that of adults over the past three decades, a new study suggests.

Moreover, the social condition of children, as measured by such markers as standardized test scores and homicide and suicide rates, has deteriorated sharply as well. The nation's overall social well-being has fallen to its lowest point since 1970, according to a Fordham University professor.

Marc L. Miringoff, the director of the Fordham Institute for Innovation in Social Policy, has conducted the annual survey since 1970. He tracks a wide range of federal data on 16 key social problems, including poverty, infant mortality, unemployment, child abuse, teenage suicide, school dropouts, and unemployment, and distills his findings into a single measure for each year on a scale of zero to 100. Lower scores indicate lower well-being.

For 1990, the latest year for which complete data are available, the index stood at 42, down three points from 1989. The index stood at 75 in 1970 and hit its peak at 79 in 1972. The figure has declined fairly steadily since then.

A subsection on children's health and well-being showed a decline for the fifth year in a row to a record low of 44 in 1990. That index hit its peak, 78, in 1976.

Skyrocketing increases in reported child abuse, the number of children living in poverty, and the number of teenage deaths by homicide fueled the falling index. (*Education Week*, 1992b, p. 3)

One thread of these environmental phenomena is composed of demographic shifts that threaten "our national standard of living and democratic foundations" (Carnegie Council on Adolescent Development, 1989, p. 27) and promise to overwhelm schools as they are now constituted. Minority enrollment in America's schools is rising, as is the proportion of less advantaged youngsters. There is a rapid increase in the number of students whose primary language is one other than English. The traditional two-parent family, with one parent employed and the other at home to care for the children, has become an anomaly, constituting only one fourth of American families (Cohen, 1992a). A few citations from educational literature convey the extent of these demographic changes:

Overall, more than 30 percent of students in public schools—
some 12 million—are now minority. (Quality Education for
Minorities Project, 1990, p. 11)

By the year 2000, . . . nearly half of all school-aged children
will be non-white. (Carnegie Council on Adolescent Development, 1989, p. 27)

Forty-six percent of children live in homes where both or the
only parent is working . . . about one half of all children and
youth will live in a single parent family for some period of
their lives. (Kirst, McLaughlin, & Massell, 1989, p. 4)

The report of the 1990 Census also documented that immigration has had a greater impact on the nation during the
1980's than in any other decade since the turn of the century.
(Schmidt, 1992, p. 9)

The share of children with mothers in the workplace rose
from 39 percent in 1970 to 61 percent in 1990, and that one in
five children—almost 13 million—live in a single-parent
home, more than twice the share 20 years ago.
     About 10 percent of children under 18 live with other rel-
atives, neighbors, friends, or in institutions. (Cohen, 1992b,
p. 14)

Between 1960 and 1987, the number of families headed by
females with children under 18 tripled. (Wagstaff & Gallagher, 1990, p. 103)

At the same time that these new threads are being woven into
the tapestry of American society, a serious unraveling of other parts
of that fabric is occurring. The number of youngsters affected by the
ills of the world in which they live—for example, poverty, unemployment, crime, drug addiction, malnutrition—is increasing, as is the
need for a variety of more intensive and extended services from
societal organizations, especially schools:

The percentage of children living in poverty in the United
States is more than double that of other major industrialized
nations. (*Education Week*, 1993, p. 3)

The 20.6 percent poverty rate reported for children under age 18 in 1990—up from 19.6 percent in 1989—"remains higher than that for any other age group," the Census Bureau noted.

The report showed that children under age 18 in 1990 accounted for 40 percent of the poor. (Cohen, 1991, p. 4)

Between 1979 and 1990, the report says, the real median income of families with children fell by 5 percent. The average income for those in the lowest bracket fell by 12.6 percent, to $9,190. Children were the poorest group, it says, with one in five, or 12.7 million, living in poverty in 1990. (Cohen, 1992b, p. 14)

30% of children in metropolitan areas live in poverty; that will increase by a third by the year 2000. Twice as high a percentage of children aged 0-6 live in poverty as do adults aged 18-64. (Clark, 1990, p. 25)

In 1980, 2.5 million people (labeled the underclass) or 3.1 percent of all households lived in 880 urban census-tract neighborhoods where more than half of the men had worked less than 26 weeks. (Wagstaff & Gallagher, 1990, p. 105)

92 percent of the high school class of 1987 had begun drinking before graduating; of those, 56 percent had begun drinking in the 6th to 9th grades. (Carnegie Council on Adolescent Development, 1989, p. 22)

8 million, or about 40 percent, of junior- and senior-high school students drink weekly, and together consume approximately 35 percent of all the wine coolers sold in the country.

More than 3 million students say they drink alone, more than 4 million drink when they are upset, and nearly 3 million drink because they are bored. (Flax, 1991, p. 13)

Nearly 60 percent of all high school students have used alcohol during the past month, and almost 4 in 10 have had more than five drinks on a single occasion, the U.S. Centers for Disease Control reports. (*Education Week*, 1991, p. 12)

More than half of the high school class of 1985 had tried marijuana, one in six had used cocaine, and one in eight had used hallucinogens like LSD. (Wagstaff & Gallagher, 1990, p. 107)

About half of the teenagers in the United States are sexually active by the time they leave school. . . . One out of four teenage [girls] has experienced a pregnancy. (Wagstaff & Gallagher, 1990, p. 108)

One-fifth of all deaths among U.S. teenagers in 1988 were due to gunshots, while nearly half of all deaths among black male teens that year were by firearms. (M. Lawton, 1991, p. 4)

Nearly two-thirds of elementary school teachers responding to a recent national survey believe that more of their students have health problems today than in the past, according to a report released here last week by the American Academy of Pediatrics and the National PTA.

   The 500 survey respondents estimated that, on average, 12 percent of their students last year had a problem that seriously affected their learning. Urban teachers said that fully 18 percent of their students had such problems. (Sommerfeld, 1992, p. 8)

Indicators that worsened during the 1980's, according to the study, included child poverty, births to unmarried teenagers, numbers of children living in single-parent homes, and percentage of low-birthweight babies. More youths were also required by juvenile courts to spend "formative years" away from their families, and the likelihood of a teenager's death as a result of an accident, suicide, or murder rose. (Cohen, 1992b, p. 14)

   A particularly troublesome aspect of this situation is the fact that, by and large, these are the students—low-income, minority, and disadvantaged youngsters—with whom schools have historically been the least successful (Carnegie Council on Adolescent Development, 1989) and for whom the appropriateness of producer-driven models of reform increasingly are being questioned.

Another harsh statistical conclusion is that poverty has increasingly become a black, female, [urban], and youthful condition. (Wagstaff & Gallagher, 1990, p. 104)

The Census Bureau report found that more than 40 percent of Hispanic children live in poverty, compared with just 13 percent of non-Hispanic whites. Puerto Rican children fared the worst, with nearly 58 percent falling below the poverty line. (Schmidt, 1993, p. 22)

African-American and Latino children make up 80 percent of the children living in distressed neighborhoods—a rate 12 times higher than their nonminority peers. (Cohen, 1994, p. 5)

If current trends continue, half of all black and Hispanic children will be poor by 2010, a Tufts University study concludes.

"Poverty will be the rule rather than the exception for the two largest racial and ethnic minorities in the country —and it will grow significantly among white children as well," said J. Larry Brown, the director of the Center on Hunger, Poverty, and Nutrition Policy at Tufts University. (Cohen, 1993, p. 11)

Forty-seven percent of Black and 56% of Hispanic adults are classified as functionally illiterate or marginal readers. (Astuto, 1990, p. 1)

The gap between White and minority achievement remains unbridged. . . . By third or fourth grade, minority and nonminority achievement levels begin to diverge. . . . By the middle school years, test scores show on average that minority children are a year or more behind. By the end of high school, a three- to four-year achievement gap between minority and nonminority youth has opened on tests such as the National Assessment of Educational Progress. (Quality Education for Minorities Project, 1990, pp. 17-18)

In 1989, . . . the combined SAT verbal and mathematics score for White students was still 27 percent higher than combined scores of Black students, 22 percent higher than scores of Puerto Rican students, and 15 percent higher than scores of American Indian and Mexican American students. (Quality Education for Minorities Project, 1990, p. 19)

While the problem of school violence is significant across the country, it tends to disproportionately affect low-achieving schools, and those with large minority populations, according to a survey of teachers also released last month. (Portner, 1994, p. 9)

In 1988, . . . about 15 percent of Black youth aged 15-24 had not graduated and were out of school . . . for Hispanic youth, the similar rate was nearly 36 percent, about three times the rate for White youth. (Quality Education for Minority Project, 1990, p. 18)

60% of prison inmates are dropouts. 58% of all dropouts are unemployed or receiving welfare. (Hutchins, 1988, p. 76)

The job rate for high school dropouts is dismal; of the 562,000 dropouts in 1985, 54 percent were unemployed and likely to remain so. (Wagstaff & Gallagher, 1990, p. 108)

The changing demographics of America—what Tom Joe, the director of the Center for the Study of Social Policy, calls "the many new realities of family life" (cited in Cohen, 1992a, p. 5)—are placing tremendous strains on the country's educational system. More and more of the types of students whom educators have failed to help in the past are entering our schools. Not only are educators being asked to educate them successfully, but the definition of success has been dramatically expanded; that is, higher levels of achievement are expected. Most critics see little hope that the ever-widening goals of education can be reached in the current system of schooling. One group of reformers is attempting to accommodate these demographic shifts by developing a new model of the educational enterprise—a deregulated model that offers advantages to consumers. In particular, some reformers maintain that strategies that empower parents and their children through markets can serve as an effective strategy for tackling the significant challenge to education posed by the changing social fabric (Murphy, 1993b).

## Move to a Postindustrial Society

We are in the midst of a revolution in the organization of human services. . . . The reliance, in the nineteenth century, on institutions is being replaced by a new service ideology, which emphasizes community programs and client choice. The monopoly of the state on service provision has been broken. The revolution is fueled by a critique of bureaucratic institutions that legitimizes the privatization of care, control, and now education. (Lewis, 1993, p. 84)

### Economic Dynamics

There is widespread agreement that the evolution of society from an industrial to a postindustrial era is helping to fuel the move toward market-based models of schooling. Three postindustrial dynamics, in particular, reinforce the relevance of privatization: economic, political, and organizational forces. On the economic front, there is a shift from an industrial to a service economy. "With the development of a service economy [comes] the need for new markets, as well as the need to break the state's monopoly on the delivery of human services so that private enterprises [can] expand. Enter 'deinstitutionalization,' " (Lewis, 1993, p. 84), "deregulation and privatization" (Caldwell, 1990, p. 17), and, according to some, "thinly disguised profit schemes masquerading as 'help' " (Achilles & DuVall, 1994, p. 9). According to this line of analysis, privatization is, in some ways, a type of new colonialism (Hardin, 1989)—an opportunity for the private sector to move into, and possibly gain control of, the 200-billion-dollar-a-year K-12 education enterprise (Beales & O'Leary, 1993) at the very time that traditional industrial growth opportunities are closing (Murphy, 1993a).

### Political Dynamics

Reinforcing the dynamics of the shift toward an information-based economy are important alterations in the political infrastructure of our society. At the broadest level, the evolution to the information age has fostered a renewed interest in political—as opposed to administrative—solutions to problems: "to the emphasis on managerial control, it juxtaposes an emphasis on political control" (March & Olson, 1983, p. 283). Equally important is the fact that the politics of tomorrow's world look increasingly individualistic (as opposed to collective) in form. There is a growing acceptance of the right of affected stakeholders to participate meaningfully in relevant decisions (Blumberg, 1985; Imber, 1983), as well as a renewed belief in the power of markets to pull societal institutions from the bureaucratic quagmire of professional control.

*Organizational Dynamics*

As we reported in earlier chapters, very closely aligned with the political forces noted above are serious efforts to overhaul the basic operating structure of our society's institutions—bureaucracy:

> The attack on bureaucracy has come from many angles, philosophical, social, technological, and practical. Perhaps practical difficulties [are] paramount: bureaucracies came to be seen as inefficient institutions unable to achieve their mandated purposes. Critiques suggest bureaucracies, especially those involving public monopolies, [are] perverse in their rewards, benefiting their own members more than those they were meant to serve. (S. B. Lawton, 1991, p. 10)

> The *problem*, so the argument goes—in mental health, corrections, and now education—is the very institutions we have built to handle the situation. The *solution* to our policy problems is to do away with the state hospital, the prison, and now the public school. It is the *institution* that causes the problem and must be transformed. (Lewis, 1993, p. 84)

There does not seem to be much use any longer for the core correlates of bureaucracy: Hierarchy of authority is often viewed as detrimental; impersonality is found to be incompatible with cooperative work efforts; specialization and division of labor are no longer considered to be assets; scientific management based on controlling the efforts of subordinates is judged to be inappropriate; and the distinct separation of management and labor is seen as counterproductive. To many, privatization is seen as the central antidote to these dysfunctions.

## The Struggle to Reinvent Education

What has come into question, it would seem, is the very legitimacy of existing educational systems. . . . There are doubts that the "technology" of teaching and school administration is adequate to meet current challenges. (S. B. Lawton, 1991, p. 3)

In addition to the environmental forces noted earlier, demands for the implementation of market-based solutions to education's problems are forming closer to the educational sector as well. There is a widespread feeling afoot that a significant restructuring of education is in order, and that major changes are needed in the systems employed to govern and manage schools and in the way we think about learning and teaching. It is also being suggested more often that the implementation of privatization arrangements in education will greatly facilitate this transformational work. Thus, a number of school-related dynamics are pushing educators to experiment with more market-based methods of conducting business. The remainder of this section examines these school-related forces for reform. We begin by reporting how centralized responses to the environmental forces described earlier were judged to be inadequate. We then overview how the search for alternative answers led reformers to examine the more decentralized solutions found in studies of successful restructuring in the corporate sector and the more market-based reforms associated with privatization in the public sector. We close by chronicling how important dimensions of the struggle to transform education are nudging us toward a more privatized system of schooling.

### The Perceived Failure
### of Efforts to Improve Education
### by Strengthening the Public Sector

After the crisis in education first surfaced in the early 1980s, initial proposals to improve education centered primarily on raising standards by expanding centralized controls. The focus was on improving the effectiveness of what would remain essentially a publicly provided service. A state-centered, top-down model of change was employed. Prescriptions and performance measurements were emphasized. Piecemeal efforts were undertaken to repair the existing educational system (Murphy, 1990). A variety of stakeholders found these approaches to be philosophically misguided and conceptually limited (Boyd, 1987; Combs, 1988; Cuban, 1984; Passow, 1984). A number of critics maintained that the standards-raising movement simply enhanced the site (and district) bureaucracy.

Subsequent efforts to address the deep-seated problems confronting education discussed above turned to more locally focused and bottom-up approaches. Enhanced professionalization and alterations to the prevailing governance structure of schooling, especially the use of shared decision making and management, have been endorsed by many reformers. An overhaul of the core technology of education consistent with student-centered and constructivist perspectives of learning and teaching has also been widely advocated (Murphy, 1991). These second wave strategies (Murphy, 1990) are different in many ways from the earlier top-down initiatives, but they are similar in one critical aspect: They both are designed to improve education by improving the performance of the public sector. Although the jury is still out on the effectiveness of these later reform strategies, there is considerable skepticism that many of them will produce desired results (Murphy, 1991; Murphy & Beck, 1995). Thus, analysts continue to search for alternative frameworks to improve the education students receive. In particular, efforts are being marshaled by some reformers to jettison "public sector improvement strategies"—and in some cases, politics altogether (Fuhrman, 1994)—in favor of approaches that highlight the employment of market forces.

### The Search for Alternative Solutions

The search for alternative solutions to the problems confronting education has led many analysts to two sources of information: knowledge about restructuring in the corporate sector and the literature on privatization of public sector services outside of education.

#### Lessons From the Corporate World

Advocates for privatizing education have found support for fundamentally different methods of operation from modern management theory and from deregulation activities in the private sector (Association for Supervision and Curriculum Development, 1986; Schlechty, 1990; Thompson, 1988). Faced with a series of problems not unlike those confronting schools—diminished product quality, inefficiencies, unhappy consumers—businesses looked inward to see how the most successful of their group were operating. By and large, it was discovered that the most effective corporations had transformed their businesses by deregulating and decentralizing operations: pushing decisions down to the level of the organization in closest contact with the consumer, reorienting their management philosophy from control to empowerment, establishing scrupulous reputations for attention to quality, and reducing the size of corporate offices and contracting out for services traditionally provided in house (Beare, 1989; Maccoby, 1989). In short, they had restructured themselves from more hierarchically organized, producer focused units to more consumer-oriented systems. These lessons are now being held up to schools (Bernas, 1992), especially by corporate managers (Gerstner, 1994; Kearnes, 1988a, 1988b), as blueprints for educational reform. Not surprisingly, given our long history of infatuation with the corporate world (Callahan, 1962; Tyack, 1993) and the severity of the crisis confronting education, there is considerable "pressure for education to adapt and incorporate current business practices" (Goldman, Dunlap, & Conley, 1991, p. 1), "to emulate leading corporations" (Ogawa, 1992, p. 19), and to reinvent schooling consistent with these "innovative management theories" (Short & Greer, 1989, p. 8).

*The Larger Privatization
Movement in the Public Sector*

In Chapters 4 and 5, we devoted considerable space to unpacking the rationale for the growth of privatization throughout the public sector. It is worth making explicit here what must be obvious. That is, these more general forces also create a very firm platform for the privatization of the educational enterprise. In a similar vein, the success with which privatization strategies have taken root in other public sectors, especially the recent spread of privatization initiatives into the social services (De Hoog, 1984), has provided a sense of the possibilities for similar activities in the educational arena. Finally, the benefits these privatization strategies have achieved in some areas in helping control costs and reach other important objectives offer considerable material to buttress the case for the use of privatization efforts in education.

## The Struggle to Transform Schooling

Around the middle of the twentieth century, we entered the post-industrial information age, a new stage in the human evolution. This new age requires new thinking, new perspectives, and a new vision of education. Improving our educational system, which is still grounded in the industrial revolution of the late nineteenth century, will not do in this postindustrial information society. What we need is a new image of education attained by a broad sweep of a comprehensive transformation—a metamorphosis. (Banathy, 1988, p. 51)

As is the case with other organizations, schools are currently engaged in a struggle to transform the way they think and act. From the collective effort of those who describe this change, a new vision of education quite unlike the "center of production" (Barth, 1986, p. 295) image that has shaped schooling throughout the industrial age is being portrayed. Embedded in this emerging view of tomorrow's schools are a number of alterations, two of which are central here: (a) at the institutional level, a change from professional to lay control; and (b) at the managerial level, a change from a bureaucratic operational system to more entrepreneurial views of schooling (Murphy, 1991, 1992a, 1992b). Both of these fundamental shifts push schools to adopt more localized and more market-sensitive methods of operating. Both add fuel to the drive to privatize education.

### Reinventing Governance

Most analysts of the institutional level of schooling—the interface of the school with its larger (generally immediate) environment—argue that the public monopoly approach to education led to "the belief in almost complete separation of schools from the community and, in turn, discouragement of local community involvement in decision making related to the administration of schools" (Burke, 1992, p. 33). Indeed, a considerable body of literature suggests that one of the major functions of bureaucracy is the buffering of the school from the environment, especially from parents and community members (Meyer & Rowan, 1975).

Many chroniclers of the changing governance structures in restructuring schools envision the demise of schooling as a sheltered government monopoly heavily controlled by professionals. In its stead, they forecast the emergence of a system of schooling and, more important for our purposes here, improvement designs driven by economic and political forces that substantially increase the saliency of the market. Embedded in this conception are a number of interesting dynamics, all of which gain force from a realignment of power and influence between professional educators and consumers. The most important is that the traditional dominant relationship—with professional educators on the playing field and parents on the sidelines acting as cheerleaders or agitators, or, more likely, passive spectators—is replaced by rules that benefit the consumer.

Four elements of this emerging portrait of transformed governance for consumers are most prevalent: choice in selecting a school, voice in school governance, partnership in the education of their children, and enhanced membership in the school community. Central to all four is a blurring of the boundaries between the home and the school, between the school and the community, and between professional staff and lay constituents (Goldring, 1992). Collectively, these components lend support to the grassroots political and competitive economic arguments that support the calls for more locally controlled organizations and to market-anchored conceptions of schooling (Murphy, 1991).

*Reinventing Systems of Administration*

What we reported in a general way about the rationale for privatization in previous chapters takes on specificity within the context of education. That is, "in recent years, critics have argued that the reforms of the Progressive Era produced bureaucratic arteriosclerosis, insulation from parents and patrons, and the low productivity of a declining industry protected as a quasi monopoly" (Tyack, 1993, p. 3). There is growing sentiment that the existing structure of administration is "obsolete and unsustainable" (Rungeling &

Glover, 1991, p. 415), and that the "bureaucratic structure is failing in a manner so critical that adaptations will not forestall its collapse" (Clark & Meloy, 1989, p. 293). Behind this basic critique lie several beliefs: that central office staff are too numerous (Viadero, 1993) and too "far removed from the schools to know and understand children and their needs" (Wagstaff & Reyes, 1993, p. 25)—beliefs often "emphasizing the incompetence of district administrators" (Garms, Guthrie, & Pierce, 1978, p. 290)—and that "bureaucracies are set up to serve the adults that run them and in the end, the kids get lost in the process" (Daly, cited in Olson, 1992, p. 10) (see also Diegmueller, 1994; Harp, 1993). It is increasingly being concluded that the existing public monopoly and its bureaucratic system of administration is "incapable of addressing the technical and structural shortcomings of the public educational system" (S. B. Lawton, 1991, p. 4).

More finely grained criticism of the bureaucratic infrastructure of schooling comes from a variety of quarters. There are those who contend that schools are so paralyzed by the "bureaucratic arteriosclerosis" noted above by Tyack (1993, p. 3) that "professional judgment" (Hill & Bonan, 1991, p. 65), "innovation and creativity" (Lindelow, 1981, p. 98), "morale" (David, 1989, p. 45), and responsibility have all been paralyzed (Bolin, 1989; Conley, 1989; Frymier, 1987; Sizer, 1984). Other reformers maintain "that school bureaucracies, as currently constituted could [never] manage to provide high-quality education" (Elmore, 1993, p. 37) and that, even worse, "bureaucratic management practices have been causing unacceptable distortions in educational process" (Wise, 1989, p. 301), that they are "paralyzing American education . . . [and] getting in the way of children's learning" (Sizer, 1984, p. 206) (see also Cuban, 1989; McNeil, 1988; Wise, 1978). Some analysts believe that bureaucracy is counterproductive to the needs and interests of educators within the school —"that it is impractical, and it does not fit the psychological and personal needs of the workforce" (Clark & Meloy, 1989, p. 293), that it "undermine[s] the authority of teachers" (Sackney & Dibski, 1992, p. 2), and that it is "incompatible with the professional organization" (Sackney & Dibski, 1992, p. 4). Still other critics suggest that bureaucratic management is inconsistent with the sacred values and purposes of education—they question "fundamental ideological issues pertaining to bureaucracy's meaning in a democratic society" (Campbell, Fleming, Newell, & Bennion, 1987, p. 73) and find that "it is inconsistent to endorse democracy in society but to be skeptical of shared governance in our schools" (Glickman, 1990, p. 74) (see also Fusarelli & Scribner, 1993). There are also scholars who view bureaucracy as a form of operation that "deflect[s] attention from the central task of teaching and learning" (Elmore, 1990, p. 5):

> Since the student is the prime producer of learning and since he is not part of the bureaucracy, and not subject to bureaucratic accountability, bureaucracy and its whole value structure must be seen as irrelevant at best, and obstructive at worst, to true learning relationships. (Seeley, 1980, p. 8)

Other reform proponents hold that the existing organizational structure of schools is neither sufficiently flexible nor sufficiently robust to meet the needs of students in a postindustrial society (D. J. Brown, 1992; Harvey & Crandall, 1988; Sizer, 1984). Finally, and most central to our work here, some analysts contend that the rigidities of bureaucracy, by making schools "almost impenetrable by citizens and unwieldy to professionals" (Candoli, 1991, p. 31), impede the ability of parents and citizens to govern and reform schooling (Campbell et al., 1987).

Not unexpectedly, given this tremendous attack on the public monopoly characteristics of schooling, stakeholders at all levels are arguing that "ambitious, if not radical, reforms are required to rectify this situation" (Elmore, 1993, p. 34), and that "the excessively centralized, bureaucratic control of . . . schools must end" (Carnegie Forum, cited in Hanson, 1991, pp. 2-3).

In its place, reformers are arguing for "a philosophy of devolved decision-making and school self-determination" (Dellar, 1992, p. 5) and "policies . . . that unleash productive local initiatives" (Guthrie, 1986, p. 306). Increasingly, they see evidence of this new philosophy in the market-anchored reform strategies of privatization.

## Conclusion

In this chapter, we shifted the frame of our analysis from the public sector in general to schooling specifically. Our intent was to track the forces fueling the privatization movement in education—forces supplementing the general political, managerial, and economic conditions outlined in Chapters 4 and 5.

We saw how privatization initiatives have gained a following as earlier reform efforts—efforts that attempted to address the crisis in student performance and the changing environment of schooling by enhancing the capacity and productivity of the public sector—have proven less than satisfactory. We also examined how the privatization movement is drawing strength from (a) central dimensions of the larger reform agenda, especially the overhaul of existing governance structures and the reinvention of the management infrastructure of schooling; and (b) the privatization efforts under way in other areas of public service delivery and analog initiatives (such as contracting out and deregulation) in the private sphere.

## Note

1. Chapter 6 is taken primarily from J. Murphy and L. G. Beck, *School-Based Management as School Reform: Taking Stock,* Corwin Press, 1995, and is used with the permission of the publisher.

# REFERENCES

Achilles, C. M., & DuVall, L. (1994, August). *Society's tectonic plates will move: Will education's?* Paper presented at the annual conference of Professors of Educational Administration, Indian Wells, CA.

American Enterprise Institute for Public Policy Research. (1970). *U.S. government finances: A 22-year perspective, 1950-1971.* Washington, DC: Author.

Aronson, J. R., & Hilley, J. L. (1986). *Financing state and local government* (4th ed.). Washington, DC: Brookings Institution.

Ascher, K. (1991). The business of local government. In R. L. Kemp (Ed.), *Privatization: The provision of public services by the private sector* (pp. 297-304). Jefferson, NC: McFarland.

Association for Supervision and Curriculum Development. (1986, September). *School reform policy: A call for reason.* Alexandria, VA: Author.

Astuto, T. A. (1990, September). *Reinventing school leadership* (Working memo prepared for the Reinventing School Leadership Conference, pp. 1-5). Cambridge, MA: National Center for Educational Leadership.

Baber, W. F. (1987). Privatizing public management: The Grace Commission and its critics. In S. H. Hanke (Ed.), *Prospects for privatization: Proceedings of the Academy of Political Science* (Vol. 36, No. 3, pp. 153-163). Montpelier, VT: Capital City Press.

Bahl, R. (1984). *Financing state and local government in the 1980s.* New York: Oxford University Press.

Bailey, R. W. (1987). Uses and misuses of privatization. In S. H. Hanke (Ed.), *Prospects for privatization: Proceedings of the Academy of Political Science* (Vol. 36, No. 3, pp. 138-152). Montpelier, VT: Capital City Press.

Bailey, R. W. (1991). Uses and misuses. In R. L. Kemp (Ed.), *Privatization: The provision of public services by the private sector* (pp. 233-249). Jefferson, NC: McFarland.

Banathy, B. H. (1988). An outside-in approach to design inquiry in education. In Far West Laboratory for Educational Research and Development (Ed.), *The redesign of education: A collection of papers concerned with comprehensive educational reform* (Vol. 1, pp. 51-71). San Francisco: Far West Laboratory.

Barth, R. S. (1986). On sheep and goats and school reform. *Phi Delta Kappan, 68*(4), 293-296.

Beales, J. R., & O'Leary, J. O. (1993, November). *Making schools work: Contracting options for better management.* Los Angeles: Reason Foundation.

Beare, H. (1989, September). *Educational administration in the 1990s.* Paper presented at the national conference of the Australian Council for Educational Administration, Armidale, New South Wales.

Bell, P., & Cloke, P. (1990). Concepts of privatisation and deregulation. In P. Bell & P. Cloke (Eds.), *Deregulation and transport: Market forces in the modern world* (pp. 3-27). London: David Fulton.

Bennett, J. T., & DiLorenzo, T. J. (1987). In S. H. Hanke (Ed.), *Prospects for privatization: Proceedings of the Academy of Political Science* (Vol. 36, No. 3, pp. 14-23). Montpelier, VT: Capital City Press.

Bennett, J. T., & Johnson, M. H. (1980). Tax reduction without sacrifice: Private-public production of public services. *Public Finance Quarterly, 8,* 363-396.

Bernas, T. G. (1992, April). *Documenting the implementation of school based management/shared decision making in a non-Chapter 1 elementary school.* Paper presented at the annual meeting of the American Educational Research Association, San Francisco.

Berry, W. D., & Lowery, D. L. (1987). *Understanding United States government growth: An empirical analysis of postwar growth.* New York: Praeger.

Blumberg, A. (1985). *The school superintendent: Living with conflict.* New York: Teachers College Press.

Bolin, F. S. (1989). Empowering leadership. *Teachers College Record, 19*(1), 81-96.

Borcherding, T. E. (1977a). One hundred years of public spending, 1870-1970. In T. E. Borcherding (Ed.), *Budgets and bureaucrats: The sources of government growth* (pp. 19-44). Durham, NC: Duke University Press.

Borcherding, T. E. (1977b). The sources of growth of public expenditures in the United States, 1902-1970. In T. E. Borcherding (Ed.), *Budgets and bureaucrats: The sources of government growth* (pp. 45-70). Durham, NC: Duke University Press.

Boyd, W. L. (1987). Public education's last hurrah? Schizophrenia, amnesia, and ignorance in school politics. *Educational Evaluation and Policy Analysis, 9*(2), 85-100.

Bradford, M. A., Malt, R. A., & Oates, E. (1969). The rising cost of local public service. *National Tax Journal, 22,* 185-202.

Brazer, H. E. (1981). On tax limitation. In N. Walzer & D. L. Chicoine (Eds.), *Financing state and local governments in the 1980s.* Cambridge, MA: Oelgeschlager, Gunn & Hain.

Brown, B. W. (1992). Why governments run schools. *Economics of Education Review, 11,* 287-300.

Brown, D. J. (1992). The recentralization of school districts. *Educational Policy, 6,* 289-297.

Brown, S. (1991). A cautionary note. In R. L. Kemp (Ed.), *Privatization: The provision of public services by the private sector* (pp. 272-275). Jefferson, NC: McFarland.

Buchanan, J. M. (1977). Why does government grow? In T. E. Borcherding (Ed.), *Budgets and bureaucrats: The sources of government growth* (pp. 3-18). Durham, NC: Duke University Press.

Buchanan, J. M. (1987). *Economics: Between predictive science and moral philosophy.* College Station: Texas A&M University Press.

Buchanan, J. M. (1989). *Essays on the political economy.* Honolulu: University of Hawaii Press.

Buchanan, J. M., & Tullock, G. (1962). *The calculus of consent: Logical foundations of constitutional democracy.* Ann Arbor: University of Michigan Press.

Burke, C. (1992). Devolution of responsibility to Queensland schools: Clarifying the rhetoric critiquing the reality. *Journal of Educational Administration, 30*(4), 33-52.

Bush, W. C., & Denzau, A. T. (1977). The voting behavior of bureaucrats and public sector growth. In T. E. Borcherding (Ed.), *Budgets and bureaucrats: The sources of government growth* (pp. 90-99). Durham, NC: Duke University Press.

Butler, S. (1991). Privatization for public purposes. In W. T. Gormley (Ed.), *Privatization and its alternatives* (pp. 17-24). Madison: University of Wisconsin Press.

Butler, S. M. (1987). Changing the political dynamics of government. In S. H. Hanke (Ed.), *Prospects for privatization. Proceedings of the Academy of Political Science* (Vol. 36, No. 3, pp. 4-13). Montpelier, VT: Capital City Press.

Caldwell, B. (1990). School-based decision-making and management: International developments. In J. Chapman (Ed.), *School-based decision-making and management* (pp. 3-26). London: Falmer.

Callahan, R. E. (1962). *Education and the cult of efficiency: A study of the social forces that have shaped the administration of the public schools.* Chicago: University of Chicago Press.

Campbell, R. F., Fleming, T., Newell, L., & Bennion, J. W. (1987). *A history of thought and practice in educational administration.* New York: Teachers College Press.

Candoli, I. C. (1991). *School system administration: A strategic plan for site-based management.* Lancaster, PA: Technomic.

Candoy-Sekse, R. (1988). *Techniques of privatization of state-owned enterprises: Vol. 3. Inventory of country experiences and reference materials.* Washington, DC: World Bank.

Carnegie Council on Adolescent Development. (1989). *Turning points.* Washington, DC: Author.

Carnegie Forum on Education and the Economy. (1986, May). *A nation prepared: Teachers for the 21st century.* Washington, DC: Author.

Carroll, B. J., Conant, R. W., & Easton, T. A. (1987). Introduction. In B. J. Carroll, R. W. Conant, & T. A. Easton (Eds.), *Private means, public ends: Private business in social service delivery* (pp. ix-xiii). New York: Praeger.

Chapman, J. (1990). School-based decision-making and management: Implications for school personnel. In C. Chapman (Ed.),

*School-based decision-making and management* (pp. 221-244). London: Falmer.

Clark, D. L. (1990, September). *Reinventing school leadership* (Working memo prepared for the Reinventing School Leadership Conference, pp. 25-29). Cambridge, MA: National Center for Educational Leadership.

Clark, D. L., & Meloy, J. M. (1989). Renouncing bureaucracy: A democratic structure for leadership in schools. In T. J. Sergiovanni & J. A. Moore (Eds.), *Schooling for tomorrow: Directing reform to issues that count* (pp. 272-294). Boston: Allyn & Bacon.

Clarkson, K. W. (1989). Privatization at the state and local level. In P. W. MacAvoy, W. T. Stanbury, G. Yarrow, & R. J. Zeckhauser (Eds.), *Privatization and state-owned enterprises: Lessons from the United States, Great Britain and Canada* (pp. 143-194). Boston: Kluwer.

Cohen, D. L. (1991). Inordinate share of poverty said to rest on children. *Education Week, 11*(6), 1.

Cohen, D. L. (1992a). Children without "traditional family" support seen posing complex challenge for schools. *Education Week, 12*(8), 5.

Cohen, D. L. (1992b). Nation found losing ground on measures of child well-being. *Education Week, 12*(28), 14.

Cohen, D. L. (1993). Half of Black, Hispanic children may be poor by 2010. *Education Week, 8*(9), 11.

Cohen, D. L. (1994). "Distressed" communities jeopardize children's well-being, report says. *Education Week, 13*(31), 5.

Combs, A. W. (1988). New assumptions for educational reform. *Educational Leadership, 45*(5), 38-40.

Committee on the Judiciary, House of Representatives. (1986). *Privatization of corrections: Hearing before the Subcommittee on Courts, Civil Liberties, and the Administration of Justice* (Serial No. 40). Washington, DC: Government Printing Office.

Conley, S. C. (1989, March). *Who's on first? School reform, teacher participation, and the decision-making process.* Paper presented at the annual meeting of the American Educational Research Association, San Francisco.

Cuban, L. (1984). School reform by remote control: SB813 in California. *Phi Delta Kappan, 66,* 213-215.

Cuban, L. (1989). The "at-risk" label and the problem of urban school reform. *Phi Delta Kappan, 70,* 780-784, 799.

Darr, T. B. (1991). Privatization may be good for your government. In R. L. Kemp (Ed.), *Privatization: The provision of public services by the private sector* (pp. 60-68). Jefferson, NC: McFarland.

David, J. L. (1989, May). Synthesis of research on school-based management. *Educational Leadership, 46*(8), 45-53.

De Alessi, L. (1987). Property rights and privatization. In S. H. Hanke (Ed.), *Prospects for privatization: Proceedings of the Academy of Political Science* (Vol. 36, No. 3, pp. 24-35). Montpelier, VT: Capital City Press.

De Hoog, R. H. (1984). *Contracting out for human services: Economic, political, and organizational perspectives.* Albany: State University of New York Press.

Dellar, G. B. (1992, April). *Connections between macro and micro implementation of educational policy: A study of school restructuring in Western Australia.* Paper presented at the annual meeting of the American Educational Research Association, San Francisco.

Diegmueller, K. (1994). Inequities lead to dual system in N.Y., panel finds. *Education Week, 13*(16), 14.

Donahue, J. D. (1989). *The privatization decision: Public ends, private means.* New York: Basic Books.

Downs, A. (1967). *Inside bureaucracy.* Boston: Little, Brown.

Dudek & Company. (1989). *Privatization and public employees: The impact of city and county contracting out on government works* (Report No. NCEP-RR-88-07). Washington, DC: U.S. National Commission for Employment Policy.

Education Commission of the States. (1983). *Action for excellence.* Denver: Author.

Education Week. (1991). Drinking among teenagers widespread, C.D.C. says. *Education Week, 11*(6), 12.

Education Week. (1992a). Community-foundation official touts new coalition on children. *Education Week, 11*(19), 6-7.

Education Week. (1992b). Dimensions: Social well-being. *Education Week, 12*(7), 3.

Education Week. (1993). Dimensions: Children in poverty. *Education Week, 13*(4), 3.

Elkin, N. (1987). Privatization in perspective. In B. J. Carroll, R. W. Conant, & T. A. Easton (Eds.), *Private means, public ends: Private business in social service delivery* (pp. 171-177). New York: Praeger.

Elmore, R. (1990). Introduction: On changing the structure of public schools. In R. Elmore & Associates (Eds.), *Restructuring schools: The next generation of educational reforms* (pp. 1-29). San Francisco: Jossey-Bass.

Elmore, R. F. (1993). School decentralization: Who gains? Who loses? In J. Hannaway & M. Carnoy (Eds.), *Decentralization and school improvement* (pp. 33-54). San Francisco: Jossey-Bass.

Fitzgerald, M. R., Lyons, W., & Cory, F. C. (1990). From administration to oversight: Privatization and its aftermath in a southern city. In R. C. Hula (Ed.), *Market-based public policy* (pp. 69-83). New York: St. Martin's.

Fitzgerald, R. (1988). *When government goes private: Successful alternatives to public services.* New York: Universe Books.

Fixler, F. L., & Poole, R. W. (1987). Status of state and local privatization. In S. H. Hanke (Ed.), *Prospects for privatization. Proceedings of the Academy of Political Science* (Vol. 36, No. 3, pp. 164-178). Montpelier, VT: Capital City Press.

Fixler, P. E. (1991). Service shedding—a new option. In R. L. Kemp (Ed.), *Privatization: The provision of public services by the private sector* (pp. 39-52). Jefferson, NC: McFarland.

Fixler, P. E., & Poole, R. W. (1991). Status of local privatization. In R. L. Kemp (Ed.), *Privatization: The provision of public services by the private sector* (pp. 69-84). Jefferson, NC: McFarland.

Flax, E. (1991). Teenage-drinking study spurs questions on efficacy of drug-prevention efforts. *Education Week, 10*(39), 13.

Florestano, P. S. (1991). Considerations for the future. In R. L. Kemp (Ed.), *Privatization: The provision of public services by the private sector* (pp. 291-296). Jefferson, NC: McFarland.

Frug, J. (1991). The choice between privatization and publicization. In R. L. Kemp (Ed.), *Privatization: The provision of public services by the private sector* (pp. 305-310). Jefferson, NC: McFarland.

Frymier, J. (1987). Bureaucracy and the neutering of teachers. *Phi Delta Kappan, 69*(1), 9-14.

Fuhrman, S. (1994). Politics and systemic education reform. *CPRE Policy Briefs*, RB-12-04/94, pp. 1-7.

Fusarelli, L. D., & Scribner, J. D. (1993, October). *Site-based management and critical democratic pluralism: An analysis of promises, problems, and possibilities.* Paper presented at the annual conference of the University Council for Educational Administration, Houston.

Garms, W. I., Guthrie, J. W., & Pierce, L. C. (1978). *School finance: The economics and politics of public education.* Englewood Cliffs, NJ: Prentice Hall.

Gerstner, L. V. (1994). *Reinventing education: Entrepreneurship in America's public schools.* New York: Dutton.

Glickman, C. D. (1990). Pushing school reform to a new edge: The seven ironies of school empowerment. *Phi Delta Kappan, 71,* 68-75.

Goetz, C. J. (1977). Fiscal illusion in state and local finance. In T. E. Borcherding (Ed.), *Budgets and bureaucrats: The sources of government growth* (pp. 176-187). Durham, NC: Duke University Press.

Goldman, H., & Mokuvos, S. (1991). Dividing the pie between public and private. In R. L. Kemp (Ed.), *Privatization: The provision of public services by the private sector* (pp. 25-28). Jefferson, NC: McFarland.

Goldman, P., Dunlap, D. M., & Conley, D. T. (1991, April). *Administrative facilitation and site-based school reform projects.* Paper presented at the annual meeting of the American Educational Research Association, Chicago.

Goldring, E. B. (1992). System-wide diversity in Israel: Principals as transformational and environmental leaders. *Journal of Educational Administration, 30*(3), 49-62.

Goldring, E. B., & Sullivan, A. V. S. (1995). Privatization: Integrating private services in public schools. In P. W. Cookson & B. Schneider (Eds.), *Transforming schools* (pp. 539-562). New York: Garland.

Gomez-Ibanez, J. A., Meyer, J. R., & Luberoff, D. E. (1990). In A. H. Munnell (Ed.), *Is there a shortfall in public capital investment?* (pp. 143-174). Boston: Federal Reserve Bank of Boston.

Gormley, W. T. (1991a). The privatization controversy. In W. T. Gormley (Ed.), *Privatization and its alternatives* (pp. 3-16). Madison: University of Wisconsin Press.

Gormley, W. T. (1991b). Two cheers for privatization. In W. T. Gormley (Ed.), *Privatization and its alternatives* (pp. 307-318). Madison: University of Wisconsin Press.

Guthrie, J. W. (1986). School-based management: The next needed education reform. *Phi Delta Kappan, 68,* 305-309.

Hanke, S. H. (1985). The theory of privatization. In S. M. Butler (Ed.), *The privatization option: A strategy to shrink the size of government* (pp. 1-14). Washington, DC: The Heritage Foundation.

Hanke, S. H. (1987). Privatization versus nationalization. In S. H. Hanke (Ed.), *Prospects for privatization: Proceedings of the Academy of Political Science* (Vol. 36, No. 3, pp. 1-3). Montpelier, VT: Capital City Press.

Hanke, S. H. (1989). Privatization at the state and local level: Comment. In P. W. MacAvoy, W. T. Stanburg, G. Yarrow, & R. J. Zeckhauser (Eds.), *Privatization and state-owned enterprises* (pp. 195-202). Boston: Kluwer.

Hanke, S. H., & Dowdle, B. (1987). Privatizing the public domain. In S. H. Hanke (Ed.), *Prospects for privatization: Proceedings of the Academy of Political Science* (Vol. 36, No. 3, pp. 114-123). Montpelier, VT: Capital City Press.

Hanke, S. H., & Walters, S. J. K. (1987). Privatizing waterworks. In S. H. Hanke (Ed.), *Prospects for privatization: Proceedings of the Academy of Political Science* (Vol. 36, No. 3, pp. 104-113). Montpelier, VT: Capital City Press.

Hanson, E. M. (1991). *School-based management and educational reform: Cases in the USA and Spain.* (ERIC Document Reproduction Service No. ED 336 832)

Hardin, H. (1989). *The privatization putsch.* Halifax, Nova Scotia: The Institute for Research on Public Policy.

Harp, L. (1993). Engler's choice plan includes student grants. *Education Week, 13*(6), 1, 18.

Harvey, G., & Crandall, D. P. (1988). A beginning look at the what and how of restructuring. In C. Jenks (Ed.), *The redesign of education: A collection of papers concerned with comprehensive educational reform* (pp. 1-37). San Francisco: Far West Laboratory.

Hatry, H. P. (1991). Problems. In R. L. Kemp (Ed.), *Privatization: The provision of public services by the private sector* (pp. 262-266). Jefferson, NC: McFarland.

Hemming, R., & Mansoor, A. M. (1988). *Privatization and public enterprises* (Occasional Paper No. 56). Washington, DC: International Monetary Fund.

Hilke, J. C. (1992). *Competition in government-financed services.* New York: Quorum Books.

Hill, P. T., & Bonan, J. (1991). *Decentralization and accountability in public education.* Santa Monica, CA: RAND.

Hirsch, W. Z. (1991). *Privatizing government services: An economic analysis of contracting out by local governments.* Los Angeles: University of California, Institute of Industrial Relations.

Hula, R. C. (1990a). Preface. In R. C. Hula (Ed.), *Market-based public policy* (pp. xiii-xiv). New York: St. Martin's.

Hula, R. C. (1990b). Using markets to implement public policy. In R. C. Hula (Ed.), *Market-based public policy* (pp. 3-18). New York: St. Martin's.

Hutchins, C. L. (1988). Redesigning education. In Far West Laboratory for Educational Research and Development (Ed.), *The redesign of education: A collection of papers concerned with comprehensive educational reform* (Vol. 1, pp. 73-78). San Francisco: Far West Laboratory.

Imber, M. (1983, April). Increased decision making involvement for teachers: Ethical and practical implications. *Journal of Educational Thought, 17*(1), 36-42.

Ismael, J. S. (1988). Privatization of social services: A heuristic approach. In J. S. Ismael & Y. Vaillancourt (Eds.), *Privatization and provincial social services in Canada* (pp. 1-11). Edmonton: University of Alberta Press.

Ismael, J. S., & Vaillancourt, Y. (1988). Preface. In J. S. Ismael & Y. Vaillancourt (Eds.), *Privatization and provincial social services in Canada* (pp. vii-ix). Edmonton: University of Alberta Press.

Kearnes, D. L. (1988a). A business perspective on American schooling. *Education Week, 7*(30), 32, 34.

Kearnes, D. L. (1988b). An education recovery plan for America. *Phi Delta Kappan, 69,* 565-570.

Kemp, R. L. (1991). Introduction. In R. L. Kemp (Ed.), *Privatization: The provision of public services by the private sector* (pp. 1-21). Jefferson, NC: McFarland.

Kirst, M. W., McLaughlin, M., & Massell, D. (1989). *Rethinking children's policy: Implications for educational administration.* Stanford, CA: Stanford University, Center for Educational Research.

Kolderie, T. (1991). Two different concepts. In R. L. Kemp (Ed.), *Privatization: The provision of public services by the private sector* (pp. 250-261). Jefferson, NC: McFarland.

Kolderie, T., & Hauer, J. (1991). Contracting as an approach to public management. In R. L. Kemp (Ed.), *Privatization: The provision of public services by the private sector* (pp. 87-96). Jefferson, NC: McFarland.

Kuttner, R. (1991). The private market can't always solve public problems. In R. L. Kemp (Ed.), *Privatization: The provision of public services by the private sector* (pp. 311-313). Jefferson, NC: McFarland.

Lawton, M. (1991). Teenage males said more apt to die from gunshots than natural causes. *Education Week, 10*(26), 4.

Lawton, S. B. (1991, September). *Why restructure?* Revision of paper presented at the annual meeting of the American Educational Research Association, Chicago.

Lewis, D. A. (1993). Deinstitutionalization and school decentralization: Making the same mistake twice. In J. Hannaway & M. Carnoy (Eds.), *Decentralization and school improvement* (pp. 84-101). San Francisco: Jossey-Bass.

Lindelow, J. (1981). School-based management. In S. C. Smith, J. A. Mazzarella, & P. K. Picle (Eds.), *School leadership: Handbook for survival* (pp. 94-129). Eugene: University of Oregon, ERIC Clearing House on Educational Management.

Maccoby, M. (1989, December). *Looking for leadership now.* Paper presented at the National Center for Educational Leadership conference, Harvard University, Cambridge, MA.

Malen, B., Ogawa, R. T., & Kranz, J. (1989, May). *What do we know about school based management? A case study of the literature—a call for research.* Paper presented at the Conference on Choice and Control in American Education, Madison, WI.

March, J. G., & Olson, J. P. (1983). What administrative reorganization tells us about governing. *American Political Science Review, 77*(2), 281-296.

Martin, B. (1993). *In the public interest? Privatization and public sector reform.* London: Zed.

Maxwell, J. A., & Aronson, J. R. (1977). *Financing state and local governments* (3rd ed.). Washington, DC: Brookings Institution.

McLaughlin, J. M. (1995). Wilkinsburg, Pennsylvania: History in the making. *Education Investor, 3*(3), 1-3.

McNeil, L. M. (1988). Contradictions of control, part 1: Administrators and teachers. *Phi Delta Kappan, 69,* 333-339.

Meltzer, A. H., & Scott, R. F. (1978, Summer). Why government grows (and grows) in a democracy. *The Public Interest, 52,* 111-118.

Meyer, J. W., & Rowan, B. (1975). *Notes on the structure of educational organizations: Revised version.* Paper presented at the annual meeting of the American Sociological Association, San Francisco.

Miller, J. R., & Tufts, C. R. (1991). A means to achieve "more with less." In R. L. Kemp (Ed.), *Privatization: The provision of public services by the private sector* (pp. 97-109). Jefferson, NC: McFarland.

Mojkowski, C., & Fleming, D. (1988). *School-site management: Concepts and approaches.* Andover, MA: Regional Laboratory for the Educational Improvement of the Northeast and Islands.

Moore, S. (1987). Contracting out: A painless alternative to the budget cutter's knife. In S. H. Hanke (Ed.), *Prospects for privatization: Proceedings of the Academy of Political Science* (Vol. 36, No. 3, pp. 60-70). Montpelier, VT: Capital City Press.

Mueller, D. C. (1989). *Public choice II.* New York: Cambridge University Press.

Murphy, J. (1990). The educational reform movement of the 1980s: A comprehensive analysis. In J. Murphy (Ed.), *The reform of American public education in the 1980s: Perspectives and cases* (pp. 3-55). Berkeley, CA: McCutchan.

Murphy, J. (1991). *Restructuring schools: Capturing and assessing the phenomena.* New York: Teachers College Press.

Murphy, J. (1992a). *The landscape of leadership preparation: Reframing the education of school administrators.* Newbury Park, CA: Corwin.

Murphy, J. (1992b). School effectiveness and school restructuring: Contributions to educational improvement. *School Effectiveness and School Improvement, 3,* 90-109.

Murphy, J. (1993a). Restructuring: In search of a movement. In J. Murphy & P. Hallinger (Eds.), *Restructuring schooling: Learning from ongoing efforts* (pp. 1-31). Newbury Park, CA: Corwin.

Murphy, J. (1993b). Restructuring schooling: The equity infrastructure. *School Effectiveness and School Improvement, 4,* 111-130.

Murphy, J., & Beck, L. G. (1995). *School-based management as school reform: Taking stock.* Thousand Oaks, CA: Corwin.

Musgrave, R. A., & Musgrave, P. B. (1976). *Public finance in theory and practice* (2nd ed.). New York: McGraw-Hill.

Nankani, L. T. (1988). *Techniques of privatization of state-owned enterprises: Vol. 2. Selected country case studies.* Washington, DC: World Bank.

National Commission on Excellence in Education. (1983). *A nation at risk: The imperative of educational reform.* Washington, DC: Government Printing Office.

National Science Board. (1983). *Educating Americans for the 21st century.* Washington, DC: Author.

Niskanen, W. A. (1971). *Bureaucracy and representative government.* Chicago: Aldine-Atherton.

Niskanen, W. A. (1994). *Bureaucracy and public economics.* Brookfield, VT: Edward Elgar.

Oates, W. E. (1972). *Fiscal federalism.* New York: Harcourt Brace Jovanovich.

Ogawa, R. T. (1992, April). *The institutional sources of educational reform: The case of school-based management.* Paper presented at the Thirteenth National Graduate Student Research Seminar in Educational Administration, San Francisco.

Olson, L. (1992). A matter of choice: Minnesota puts "charter schools" idea to test. *Education Week, 12*(12), 1, 10-11.

Pack, J. R. (1991). The opportunities and constraints of privatization. In W. T. Gormley (Ed.), *Privatization and its alternatives* (pp. 281-306). Madison: University of Wisconsin Press.

Passow, A. H. (1984). *Reforming schools in the 1980s: A critical review of the national reports.* New York: Columbia University, Teachers College, Institute for Urban and Minority Education.

Peirce, W. S. (1981). *Bureaucratic failure and public expenditure.* New York: Academic Press.

Peters, T. (1991). Public services and the private sector. In R. L. Kemp (Ed.), *Privatization: The provision of public services by the private sector* (pp. 53-59). Jefferson, NC: McFarland.

Phares, D. (1981). The fiscal status of the state-local sector: A look to the 1980s. In N. Walzer & D. L. Chicoine (Eds.), *Financing state and local governments in the 1980s: Issues and trends* (pp. 145-173). Cambridge, MA: Oelgeschlager, Gunn & Hain.

Pines, B. Y. (1985). The conservative agenda. In S. M. Butler (Ed.), *The privatization option: A strategy to shrink the size of government* (p. v). Washington, DC: The Heritage Foundation.

Pirie, M. (1985). The British experience. In S. M. Butler (Ed.), *The privatization option: A strategy to shrink the size of government* (pp. 51-68). Washington, DC: The Heritage Foundation.

Pirie, M. (1988). *Privatization.* Hants, UK: Wildwood House.

Poole, R. (1985). The politics of privatization. In S. M. Butler (Ed.), *The privatization option: A strategy to shrink the size of government* (pp. 33-50). Washington, DC: The Heritage Foundation.

Portner, J. (1994). School violence up over past 5 years, 82% in survey say. *Education Week, 13*(16), 9.

President's Commission on Privatization. (1988). *Privatization: Toward more effective government.* Washington, DC: Government Printing Office.

Quality Education for Minorities Project. (1990). *Education that works: An action plan for the education of minorities.* Cambridge: MIT Press.

Ramsey, J. B. (1987). Selling the New York City subway: Wild-eyed radicalism or the only feasible solution. In S. H. Hanke (Ed.), *Prospects for privatization: Proceedings of the Academy of Political Science* (Vol. 36, No. 3, pp. 93-103). Montpelier, VT: Capital City Press.

Renner, T. (1989, November/December). Trends and issues in the use of intergovernmental agreements and privatization in local government. *Baseline Data Report, 21*(6). Washington, DC: International City Management Association.

Roehm, H. A., Castellano, J. F., & Karns, D. A. (1991). In R. L. Kemp (Ed.), *Privatization: The provision of public services by the private sector* (pp. 276-288). Jefferson, NC: McFarland.

Rose, R. (1984). *Understanding big government: The programme approach.* London: Sage.

Ross, R. L. (1988). *Government and the private sector: Who should do what?* New York: Crane Russak.

Roth, G. (1987). Airport privatization. In S. H. Hanke (Ed.), *Prospects for privatization: Proceedings of the Academy of Political Science* (Vol. 36, No. 3, pp. 74-82). Montpelier, VT: Capital City Press.

Rungeling, B., & Glover, R. W. (1991). Educational restructuring—the process for change? *Urban Education, 25,* 415-427.

Sackney, L. E., & Dibski, D. J. (1992, August). *School-based management: A critical perspective.* Paper presented at the Seventh Regional Conference of the Commonwealth Council for Educational Administration, Hong Kong.

Savas, E. S. (1982). *Privatizing the public sector: How to shrink government.* Chatham, NJ: Chatham House.

Savas, E. S. (1985). The efficiency of the private sector. In S. M. Butler (Ed.), *The privatization option: A strategy to shrink the size of government* (pp. 15-31). Washington, DC: The Heritage Foundation.

Savas, E. S. (1987). *Privatization: The key to better government.* Chatham, NJ: Chatham House.

Schlechty, P. C. (1990). *Schools for the 21st century: Leadership imperatives for educational reform.* San Francisco: Jossey-Bass.

Schmidt, P. (1992). Census data find more are falling behind in school. *Education Week, 11*(38), 1, 9.

Schmidt, P. (1993). Hispanic poverty said linked to lack of education. *Education Week, 13*(1), 22.

Scully, L. J., & Cole, L. A. (1991). Making the decision. In R. L. Kemp (Ed.), *Privatization: The provision of public services by the private sector* (pp. 110-121). Jefferson, NC: McFarland.

Seader, D. (1991). Privatization and America's cities. In R. L. Kemp (Ed.), *Privatization: The provision of public services by the private sector* (pp. 29-38). Jefferson, NC: McFarland.

Seeley, D. S. (1980, February). *The bankruptcy of service delivery.* Presentation delivered before the Foundation Lunch Group: Panel on Children at the Edwin Gould Foundation for Children, New York.

Seldon, A. (1987). Public choice and the choices of the public. In C. K. Rowley (Ed.), *Democracy and public choice* (pp. 122-134). New York: Columbia University Press.

Shannon, J. (1981). The slowdown in the growth of state-local spending: Will it last? In N. Walzer & D. L. Chicoine (Eds.), *Financing state and local governments in the 1980s: Issues and trends* (pp. 223-245). Cambridge, MA: Oelgeschlager, Gunn & Hain.

Short, P. M., & Greer, J. T. (1989, March). *Increasing teacher autonomy through shared governance: Effects on policy making and student outcomes.* Paper presented at the annual meeting of the American Educational Research Association, San Francisco.

Sizer, T. R. (1984). *Horace's compromise: The dilemma of the American high school*. Boston: Houghton Mifflin.

Smith, F. L. (1987). Privatization at the federal level. In S. H. Hanke (Ed.), *Prospects for privatization: Proceedings of the Academy of Political Science* (Vol. 36, No. 3, pp. 179-189). Montpelier, VT: Capital City Press.

Sommerfeld, M. (1992). Survey charts rise in health problems among pupils. *Education Week, 12*(3), 8.

Starr, P. (1987). The limits of privatization. In S. H. Hanke (Ed.), *Prospects for privatization: Proceedings of the Academy of Political Science* (Vol. 36, No. 3, pp. 124-137). Montpelier, VT: Capital City Press.

Starr, P. (1991). The case for skepticism. In W. T. Gormley (Ed.), *Privatization and its alternatives* (pp. 25-36). Madison: University of Wisconsin Press.

Stiglitz, J. E. (1986). *Economics of the public sector* (2nd ed.). New York: Norton.

Tax Foundation. (1993). *Facts and figures on government finance: 1993 edition*. Washington, DC: Author.

Thayer, F. C. (1987). Privatization: Carnage, chaos, and corruption. In B. J. Carroll, R. W. Conant, & T. A. Easton (Eds.), *Private means, public ends: Private business in social service delivery* (pp. 146-170). New York: Praeger.

Thompson, F. (1989). Privatization at the state and local level: Comment. In P. W. MacAvoy, W. T. Stanbury, G. Yarrow, & R. J. Zeckhauser (Eds.), *Privatization and state-owned enterprises* (pp. 202-207). Boston: Kluwer.

Thompson, J. A. (1988). The second wave of educational reform: Implications for school leadership, administration, and organization. In F. C. Wendel & M. T. Bryant (Eds.), *New directions for administrator preparation* (pp. 9-24). Tempe, AZ: University Council for Educational Administration.

Tullock, G. (1965). *The politics of bureaucracy*. Washington, DC: Public Affairs Press.

Tullock, G. (1988). *Wealth, poverty, and politics*. New York: Basil Blackwell.

Tullock, G. (1994a). Public choice: The new science of politics. In G. L. Brady & R. D. Tollison (Eds.), *On the trail of homo economicus* (pp. 87-100). Fairfax, VA: George Mason University Press.

Tullock, G. (1994b). Social cost and government policy. In G. L. Brady & R. D. Tollison (Eds.), *On the trail of homo economicus* (pp. 65-85). Fairfax, VA: George Mason University Press.

Tyack, D. (1993). School governance in the United States: Historical puzzles and anomalies. In J. Hannaway & M. Carnoy (Eds.), *Decentralization and school improvement* (pp. 1-32). San Francisco: Jossey-Bass.

Urschel, J. (1995, May 16). Fear, distrust, suspicion of the government. *USA Today*, pp. 1-2.

Van Horn, C. E. (1991). The myths and realities of privatization. In W. T. Gormley (Ed.), *Privatization and its alternatives* (pp. 261-280). Madison: University of Wisconsin Press.

Viadero, D. (1993). Majority of education workforce found to be non-teachers. *Education Week, 13*(14), 3.

Vickers, J., & Yarrow, G. (1988). *Privatization: An economic analysis*. Cambridge: MIT Press.

Voylsteke, C. (1988). *Techniques of privatization of state-owned enterprises: Vol. 1. Methods and implementation*. Washington, DC: World Bank.

Wagstaff, L. H., & Gallagher, K. S. (1990). Schools, families, and communities: Idealized images and new realities. In B. Mitchell & L. L. Cunningham (Eds.), *Educational leadership and changing contexts of families, communities, and schools* (pp. 91-117). Chicago: University of Chicago Press.

Wagstaff, L. H., & Reyes, P. (1993, August). *School site-based management* (Report presented to the Educational Economic Policy Center). Austin: University of Texas, College of Education.

Walters, A. A. (1987). Ownership and efficiency in urban buses. In S. H. Hanke (Ed.), *Prospects for privatization: Proceedings of the Academy of Political Science* (Vol. 36, No. 3, pp. 83-92). Montpelier, VT: Capital City Press.

Wildavsky, A. (1985). Equality, spending limits, and the growth of government. In C. L. Harriss (Ed.), *Control of federal spending: Proceedings of the Academy of Political Science* (Vol. 35, No. 4, pp. 59-71). Montpelier, VT: Capital City Press.

Wilson, L. A. (1990). Rescuing politics from the economists: Privatizing the public sector. In R. C. Hula (Ed.), *Market-based public policy* (pp. 59-68). New York: St. Martin's.

Wise, A. E. (1978). The hyper-rationalization of American education. *Educational Leadership, 35,* 354-361.

Wise, A. E. (1989). Professional teaching: A new paradigm for the management of education. In T. J. Sergiovanni & J. H. Moore (Eds.), *Schooling for tomorrow: Directing reforms to issues that count* (pp. 301-310). Boston: Allyn & Bacon.

Worsnop, R. L. (1992, November). Privatization. *Congressional Quarterly Researcher, 2*(42), 977-1000.

Young, P. (1987). Privatization around the world. In S. H. Hanke (Ed.), *Prospects for privatization: Proceedings of the Academy of Political Science* (Vol. 36, No. 3, pp. 190-206). Montpelier, VT: Capital City Press.

# INDEX

CORWIN
PRESS

**The Corwin Press logo**—a raven striding across an open book— represents the happy union of courage and learning. We are a professional-level publisher of books and journals for K-12 educators, and we are committed to creating and providing resources that embody these qualities. Corwin's motto is "Success for All Learners."